"WOMEN IN BRAZIL"

CAIPORA WOMEN'S GROUP

**LATIN AMERICA
BUREAU**

First published in 1993 in the UK by the Latin America Bureau (Research and Action) Ltd, 1 Amwell Street, London EC1R 1UL

© CAIPORA

A CIP catalogue record for this book is available from the British Library

ISBN 0 906156 79 3   (pbk)
ISBN 0 906156 80 7   (hbk)

Editor: Duncan Green
Special adviser: Rebecca Reichmann
Translator: Terry Bond

Cover: Andy Dark

Typeset, printed and bound by Russell Press, Nottingham NG7 3HN
Trade distribution in UK by Central Books, 99 Wallis Road, London E9 5LN
Distribution in North America by Monthly Review Press, 122 West
27th Street, New York, NY 10001

Contents

Introduction

Salete dos Santos Gonçalves, 39 years old, is hoping that finally, after a four-year struggle, she and her family will gain a plot of land to farm in their home state of Rio Grande do Sul. At the moment, they and another 518 families are living precariously in a temporary camp, called *Não-Me-Toque* (Don't Touch Me), illegally situated on government land. Though untrained, Salete is providing the families with elementary medical care, while one of her daughters, 16-year-old Evanir, is teaching the children in the camp to read and write.

For years Salete and her husband, Sebastião, were rural workers, employed on a daily basis to harvest crops in the big farms. 'It was too much', says Salete. 'We didn't have a fair wage or a doctor for our children. There was only work for a few months of the year. We lived hopping from branch to branch'. In 1989, Salete's life changed. 'Along with 56 other families, we joined the Movement for Landless Families', comments Salete. 'Since then, we have taken part in five land invasions, all of which ended badly. We were evicted, often violently, by the police.'

In April 1993, Salete and her family took part in a Movement for Landless Families (MST) campaign involving a two-day march to the state capital, Porto Alegre. Four supporters then went on a hunger strike. After a large demonstration, the federal government finally agreed to expropriate land to settle the families living in camps. 'If God wills, we'll get a plot of land where we can all build our own homes and collectively cultivate our crops', says Salete.

Maria da Gloria Teixeira, 50 years old, lives with seven of her 18 children in a one-room shack in the shanty-town of Rio das Pedras in Jacarepagua in Rio de Janeiro. Four of her children have died. Another, 9-year-old Armindo, suffers from cerebral palsy and lies all day in a cot. The other six, from 5 to 16 years old, do all kinds of odd jobs. Together, they earn US$20-30 a month. The family survives by collecting scraps of food on rubbish tips.

A makeshift pipe brings water into Maria da Gloria's hut. The sewer is an open channel in front of the house. 'When it rains, the sewer floods and sewage gets into my water', she says. If the rains are heavy, sewage can even flood over the floor of her hut. 'Just last week', she says, 'two of my children were bitten by rats.' None of the children has been vaccinated.

Maria da Gloria and her family are some of the 40 million Brazilians estimated by the government to be living in absolute poverty. Her shack is just quarter of an hour's walk away from the luxury apartment block of Barra da Tijuca, where Brazil's rich elite enjoys one of the most glamorous life styles in the world.

Maria Alice Ferraz is one of the last employees working for Codevale (the Commission for the Development of the Valley of Jequitinhonha), a government agency set up in the 1970s to help develop an impoverished area in the north of the state of Minas Gerais. Maria, who earns US$60 a month, travels throughout the region buying up pottery. For many of the families, it is their only way of earning money. 'Like many government agencies, Codevale is in a state of collapse', says Maria. 'It has virtually closed down, except for the pottery section, which is self-financing.'

As there is little employment in the region, most of the men spend seven months of the year in the state of São Paulo, working in sugar mills. The women are left to bring up the children in extreme hardship. 'Many end up giving their children cachaça (sugar-cane rum). It is cheaper than milk and it stops them crying all night from hunger. Alcoholism does become a problem, but it's easier for the women to deal with than starvation.'

Maria do Socorro Lira Feitosa, a 32-year-old peasant woman, gathered together about 100 people from her small community in the state of Pernambuco in the drought-ridden Northeast of Brazil. Carrying candles to help them find their way at night, palm leaves to protect them from the morning sun and a little manioc flour to eat, they set out in the middle of the night to walk 24 kilometres to the cross-roads where Luis Inacio 'Lula' da Silva, president of the Workers' Party, was due to pass by the following morning. At the head of a large caravan, organised to alert the country to the problem of hunger, Lula was repeating the journey he had made 41 years earlier as a 7-year-old child, when his mother — along with hundreds of thousands of other Brazilians — had made the long trek down from the impoverished Northeast in search of a new life in the industrial city of São Paulo.

Holding a microphone, Maria do Socorro, mother of nine children, spoke to the caravan. 'We're not here to be nice', she said. 'We're here because we're starving.' In a few minutes she told the story of her community, a story of hardship, unemployment and hunger. A university lecturer taking part in the caravan was impressed by the power of her language and the force of her logic. 'I very much doubt whether the President of the Republic could have ordered his arguments more effectively', he confessed. The newspapers on the following day called her Mother Courage.

When she ended by stating emphatically: 'We are not returning on foot', everyone knew she meant it. Transport home was arranged, and Lula set up a special commission to help this small community lobby the state and federal government.

Stories like these abound throughout Brazil where thousands of women are fighting for their families and their communities, often in the most difficult conditions. Their fearlesness, tenacity and sheer guts impress all who meet them and prompted the Brazilian and German members of the Caipora women's group to put together this book, originally published in Germany in 1991. Some of the women featured in this book are heads of families, facing the world alone. Many others are the driving force in their families, living with men who, after long periods of unemployment or exhausting work for low pay, have given up the struggle. Perhaps because they lack that stubborn commitment to their children shared by so many women, Brazilian men often do not seem to measure up to the standard set by the women.

The courage shown by the women is all the more remarkable because it takes place against a background of profound inequality, for women face a range of discriminatory practices throughout society.

Poor and Rich

The most profound inequality faced by most Brazilian women is not specific to their gender. It is simply the discrimination that they suffer from being poor in a society that, to an extraordinary extent, is geared to the interests of the rich.

According to World Bank figures, Brazil is the most unequal society in the world: the richest 20 per cent of the population has an income 27.3 times greater than the poorest 20 per cent of the population. Next in the table comes Botswana, where the ratio is

23.6. In India, it is 5.1 and in Bangladesh, 3.7. Though figures are not available, most economists believe that even within Brazil's richest 20 per cent, income is highly concentrated, with a small elite enjoying one of the most sumptuous living standards in the world.

At the other end of the scale, about 14.4 million families — 65 million people — are considered 'poor', that is, they have a monthly income of half a minimum wage (US$25) or less. Over half of these — about 34 million — do not earn enough money to feed themselves adequately, even if they were able to use all their income to buy food. These are the so-called 'indigents'.

World Bank figures indicate that the situation has been getting steadily worse for those at the bottom of the heap: while the poorest 2 per cent of the population had 2.6 per cent of the wealth in 1980, their share had dropped to 2.1 per cent by 1990. In Latin America as a whole, the poorest 20 per cent had 4 per cent of the income in 1990.

One of the main reasons for the intensifying concentration of wealth is runaway inflation. Over the last 5 years Brazilian inflation reached 1,825,059,944,842.56 per cent, probably a world record. In 1992 alone it reached 1,150 per cent, second only to Russia. Brazil's inflation soars far ahead of it neighbours: in 1992 the cost-of-living index rose by 17 per cent in Argentina, 13 per cent in Chile, and 9 per cent in Bolivia. Inflation at this level acts as a powerful mechanism for transferring wealth from the poor to the rich, who can use their access to the financial system to hedge against high inflation. They can put their money in inflation-indexed savings accounts. They can open up dollar accounts abroad. They can buy up inflation-proof assets, like gold and property.

None of these tricks is available to the poor who earn the minimum wage, the value of which is only adjusted at three-monthly intervals. Whereas the minimum wage might be worth US$70-80 immediately after an increase, its value falls to about USS30-40 by the end of the period. Besides this, the adjustment fixed by the government is never enough to make up in full for the erosive impact of inflation. As a result, the purchasing power of the minimum wage has halved in the last decade.

The decline in living standards of the poor, combined with the grave crisis in the state sector, which for all practical purposes has gone bankrupt, has led to an unprecedented social crisis. About 98 million people, three-quarters of them in urban areas, have no sewers. About 30 million have no running water. Diseases, such as cholera, which the government thought eradicated for ever, have re-emerged. According to the health ministry, the country's public health system has degenerated into an enormous system of emergency medicine, with doctors and nurses treating diseases that could have been prevented earlier. An estimated 80 per cent of the people visiting casualty, and 6 per cent of the patients admitted to hospital, are suffering from illnesses that would not have arisen if the country had an adequate system of drinking water and sanitation. Other illnesses, such as malaria, that could be controlled with sufficient investment from the government, are spreading. Brazil now has 530,000 cases of malaria a year — twice the level of 1979.

Widespread poverty has also spawned an increasing number of armed robberies and murders in the cities. Though the wealthy complain vociferously about the rise in thefts, murders and kidnappings in well-off areas of the cities, it is the poor who suffer most from urban violence. Death from so-called 'external causes' (largely murder and deaths from traffic accidents) now makes up 17 per cent of deaths, compared with 5 per cent in 1979.

All this means that life is very hard for the poor, whatever their gender, but there is no doubt that women have a rougher deal than men.

Women at Work

Prejudice against women is blatant in the workplace. The number of women working in industry has more than tripled since 1970. Displacing men, they are stepping into low-skilled, low-paying, repetitive jobs clustered in the textiles and electronics industries. Women are also disproportionately represented among temporary, part-time and home-based workers.

Despite the importance of female workers in the industrial labour force, most women find it extremely difficult to have a career structure and to work their way up through the job market. They are employed as unskilled workers and there they are expected to stay. Men are selected before women for skills training and promotion, and their wages reflect this. Research carried out in 1985 showed that in São Paulo, Latin America's most advanced industrial metropolis, the average male income was more than double the average female income, at the same levels of education. The gap between the two — which, surprisingly, was greatest at the highest educational levels — was wider than anywhere else in the Americas.

Women are cheap workers, and employers are keen to keep them this way, despite the clauses in the 1988 Constitution guaranteeing equal pay for comparable work. To keep to a minimum their outlay on maternity pay and childcare, some employers conduct covert pregnancy tests during 'routine' health check-ups. Others simply demand proof of sterilisation before taking on women workers.

Despite the changes, the number of jobs available in industry for women remains limited, particularly as the Brazilian economy has been going through a decade-long recession. Many female workers, particularly black women and semi-literate women from the countryside, have to resort to the traditional source of employment for poor Brazilian women, domestic service, still responsible for about half of women's jobs. Thanks to a vigorous campaign carried out by the Trade Union of Domestic Workers, more maids are being registered by their employers at the ministry of employment, which means that they are finally gaining access to the limited welfare services available through the social services. But even so, pay is generally low and conditions of work poor.

Some women, particularly in the frontier mining zones and in the cities, cannot get jobs as maids or reject their working conditions. Many of these women turn to an even older trade — prostitution. AIDS has made this a particularly hazardous profession. Originally most prevalent among homosexual and bisexual men, AIDS is now quietly spreading among women and children. By 1993, over 34,000 cases of AIDS had been reported in Brazil, about 12,000 of them in children. Up to a million people are believed to be infected with HIV.

In response, prostitutes are getting organised, particularly in the cities. Simone, a 20-year-old in São Paulo, said that she and many of her colleagues now demand that their clients use condoms. 'Yesterday, a man offered to pay me double, if I had sex without a condom', she recalls. 'I refused.' With support from the state government, Simone and another 60 women, all of whom work in the centre of São Paulo around the Luz railway station, have just published a 15-page booklet, giving basic health information for prostitutes. They are also campaigning for a free supply of condoms. 'We charge 50,000 cruzeiros (about US$4) to have sex', says Simone. 'On pay day, we each have about six to ten customers, but on other days trade is slack. A pack of three condoms costs about 25,000 cruzeiros (about US$2). It's a big chunk out of our pay. We need a regular free supply.' In a country without an adequate system of social welfare, some Brazilian women do not have the money to bring up their children adequately. This is undoubtedly the main reason why about seven million youngsters are on the streets, earning money by selling sweets, watching over parked cars and, in a few cases, robbing passers-by. It is not just an urban phenomenon, hundreds of thousands of kids work in the countryside. One such child-worker is 14-year-old Alessandra Ribeiro, who is picked up by a truck each day at 5 a.m. from her home in Felixlandia in the interior of the state of Minas Gerais. She and 16 other girls, known as the *'meninas-formicidas'* ('the girl ant-killers'), spend all day applying insecticide with their bare hands to kill the ants that infest the eucalyptus plantation. For this, she earns about US$2 a day.

Women and Fertility

Many Brazilian women are profoundly distressed by their failure to carry out properly what they see as their basic task — to look after their children properly. Many of them are taking desperate measures to avoid having any more children. Even though it is illegal to terminate a pregnancy, except in a very few restricted circumstances, the World Health Organisation put the number of abortions in Brazil at between three and five million a year. The Brazilian Bar Association (OAB), gives an even higher estimate — about six million.

Though almost all Brazilian women of every class seem to have an abortion at some time or other in their lives, poor women going to public hospitals to be treated for post-abortion complications still face great prejudice. Maria Alice, a 48-year-old black woman, married when she was 14. She became a widow at 22, married again, but separated when she was 34. She then turned to prostitution as the only means of raising her children. As well as having 11 children, she has had 13 miscarriages and four abortions.

She says that all her attempts at abortion were dangerous and extremely unpleasant: 'The first time I wanted an abortion, in 1979, I went to a *curiosa* (a backstreet abortionist). She tried to suck out the foetus with a pump. I went to hospital with heavy bleeding but the doctor threatened to call the police. So I went back to the *curiosa*, who cleaned me out without giving me an anaesthetic. The pain was agonising.'

After such an experience, Maria Alice was unwilling to go back to the *curiosa*. 'When I needed abortions again, in 1983 and 1985, I did it all myself. I used a cabbage stalk, drank abortive teas and took Cytotec (a drug). Both times I suffered terrible pain and bled for over a week. But it worked.' Maria Alice's last abortion, in 1990, was in some ways the worst. 'I tried to do the abortion myself but had to go to hospital. They called me a murderer and left me for three days on a stretcher in the corridor. When my friends found me, I was beginning to rot inside.'

The drug taken by Maria Alice — Cytotec — is becoming increasingly popular. It was originally brought into Brazil by the drug companies to treat ulcers. One of its side effects, however, is to contract the uterus, provoking an internal haemorrhage. Though it should be sold only under prescription, Cytotec is readily available in Brazilian chemists, as are many other powerful drugs. An article published recently in the British medical magazine, *The Lancet*, gives the result of a research project carried out from 1990 to 1992 in a hospital in Fortaleza in the Northeast of the country. According to the article, 1,916 women were admitted to this hospital during this time to have uterine scrapes; 31 per cent of these women had attempted an abortion, almost three-quarters of them by taking Cytotec.

Many of the same pressures that lead Brazilian women to have abortions are also responsible for the recent rapid increase in female sterilisation. Though the government has never undertaken a national campaign in favour of sterilisation, and the Catholic Church is still opposed to it, about 30 per cent of Brazilian women of child-bearing age, including many in their late teens or early twenties, have been sterilised. It is clear that many young women see it as the lesser of two evils: it is better to be sterilised when you are 20 than to end up with ten children. Though no up-to-date statistics are available, the high level of sterilisation must be leading to a decline in abortion.

The situation worries many Brazilians. 'Our rate of female sterilisation is three times the average in developed countries and higher than in almost every other developing country', comments Senator Carlos Patrocinio, who headed a Congressional enquiry into the issue. Eva Blay, a senator who has done a great deal to increase national awareness about women's issues, points out that about one in eight women later regret the step. But, she says, the women are usually behaving responsibly, given the narrow range of options they face. 'It's largely the fault of the federal government', she says. 'While unwilling to provide a proper family planning service that allows women to make informed choices, it has allowed foreign agencies, largely from the United States, to fund sterilisation programmes. It has also turned a blind eye to the not uncommon practice, documented in the state of Pernambuco and São Paulo, of politicians paying the bills for voters' sterilisation operations in return for their votes.'

Eva Blay is now campaigning to have abortion decriminalised. She also wants the 1988 Constitution respected, as it guarantees women the right to choose between a wide range of contraceptive devices. 'They keep telling me that poor women aren't capable of using contraceptives, like the cap or the pill. That's ridiculous. They can make great cakes, for example, and that's far more complicated. See if most men can do it.'

Apart from sterilisation, the only other method of birth control commonly used in Brazil is the pill, which is freely available at chemists and is the form of contraception favoured by middle-class women. It is estimated that about 20-25 per cent of married women are on the pill.

Taken together, abortion, sterilisation and the pill have revolutionised Brazil's demographic patterns. In the 1940s, Brazilian women had on average 6.2 children. By 1980, the average had fallen to 3.5 children, declining further to 2.5 children in 1990. Even in the backward Northeast, where the Brazilian public still imagines peasant families have 11 or 12 children, the average number of children per woman fell from 5.1 in 1980 to 3.5 in 1990. As a result, Brazil's population growth rate fell from an annual average of 2.4 per cent in the 1970s to 2.2 per cent in the 1980s.

The Women's Movement

The sweeping changes that have occurred to women's lives over the last 40 or 50 years have led women in Brazil, as in many other countries in the world, to demand a greater say over what happens to them. The women's movement emerged as a political force in the 1960s and, as happened with the mass-based movements among landless peasant families and Indian communities, the Catholic Church played an important role. As many priests and lay-workers turned towards the poor and against the military regime, they promoted community organisations, especially among those who had been increasingly excluded by the post-1964 regime. Women were actively encouraged to participate.

The Catholic Church, however, did not on the whole challenge the conventional view of women's role in society. Women were usually encouraged to set up 'mothers' clubs', which were intended to deal with 'women's issues', such as child-rearing, cooking and home-building. With the growth in opposition to the military, these clubs provided the organisational base for several political movements which expanded into city-wide, and even nation-wide, political campaigns. Mothers in their clubs were the driving force behind the Women's Amnesty Movement, the Cost of Living Movement and the Fight for Creches Movement all of which had considerable political importance in the 1970s and 1980s. Even so, these movements tended not to concern themselves with the overall situation of women in society. Their action centred on demanding community day-centres and better health care services for women and children from the municipal and state governments.

The creation since the mid-1970s of specifically feminist organisations has helped to mobilise women on gender issues. There are today more than 400 feminist groups, most of them set up by middle-class women. Since the opening up of the political system in the early 1980s, these groups have played an active role within the party political system. Women lobbied heavily during the drawing up of the 1988 Constitution, establishing women's rights to four months of maternity leave, equal pay for comparable work, social security for domestic workers and title to property regardless of marital status.

Brazilian women often complain that the pace of change has been agonisingly slow, particularly if compared with the advances made in many of the industrialised countries. But Marta Suplicy, a leading sexologist, is sanguine: 'Brazilian women couldn't vote until 1932. Until 1962 they were treated under Brazilian law as equivalent to children or primitive Indians. They had to ask permission from their fathers or husbands to leave the country or even to drive a car. A lot more needs to be done, but we've come a long way.'

One of the areas where change has been occurring most rapidly is the treatment of women in the home. Domestic violence is a problem that women — and women alone — have to face. Women are still assaulted and killed with virtual impunity in crimes of passion, particularly in the countryside. Because a man's 'honour' traditionally takes precedence over a woman's rights, the so-called 'honour defence' is still successful in 80 per cent of the cases that come to court. At the same time the police almost always fail to press charges against men accused of battering or raping women in the home. All this led Americas Watch to conclude in a report published in 1991 that there was a clear pattern of discrimination against female victims of domestic violence in the Brazilian criminal justice system.

For over 20 years the women's movement has been campaigning against the failure of the Brazilian government to punish those responsible for domestic violence. Finally, in 1984, Brazil ratified the United Nations Convention on the Elimination of All Forms of

Discrimination Against Women. Shortly afterwards, it set up 79 specialised police stations to deal exclusively with crimes of violence against women. Then, after a nationwide women's rights campaign, the 1988 Constitution guaranteed the equality of women before the law and established the government's obligation to prevent violence in the home as well as in the public domain.

All this has revolutionised women's attitudes. The number of women registering complaints at the special stations has been rising rapidly. This may reflect, in part, an increase in violence, as living standards deteriorate in the sprawling urban areas around all Brazil's cities. But the rise is also thought to reflect growing determination by women to have their rights respected.

Despite these advances, the legacy of the past lingers. Many police officers, male and female, still fail to regard domestic abuse as a serious crime. Discriminatory attitudes towards female victims persist, even at the special women's stations. Many police staff still consider battering to be a private rather than a criminal offence and urge women not to register their complaints. The police also tend to hold stereotypical attitudes about women's roles, accusing women who are out alone at night of 'neglecting' their husbands and of somehow provoking violence.

Black Women

Most women in Brazil are the victims of double discrimination — for being poor and female. But there is a further large group of women who suffer a third type of discrimination — for being black. Black Brazilians account for about 45 per cent of the population. Year after year studies show that they are victims of glaring racial discrimination. Compared with white Brazilians with the same level of education and with similar work experience, black Brazilians can expect to lose more children to disease, die sooner themselves and earn less. Black Brazilians who have had 12 years of schooling earn less than white Brazilians with eight years of education.

Despite all the evidence, racial discrimination is rarely acknowledged and poorly understood, even by Brazilians themselves. Many talk of Brazil as a 'racial democracy', a concept first devised by the anthropologist, Gilberto Freyre, in the 1930s. According to him, Brazil's long history of racial miscegenation forged a common Brazilian identity that was neither 'black' nor 'white'. With all races freely intermingling, Brazil developed, he claims, a culture of racial cordiality. It was a convenient theory, readily adopted by the elite and the media, who have long dismissed racism as a preoccupation of foreigners.

The myth was exposed as early as the 1950s, when a UNESCO team found the same racial inequalities rooted in discrimination that today's demographers confirm. Despite the recent growth in black awareness, Brazilians are reluctant to admit the scale of the problem, even in left-wing circles. Benedita da Silva, the country's first black woman deputy, who ran unsuccessfully for the mayorship of Rio de Janeiro in November 1992, privately complains of racism, even in the ranks of her own party, the left-of-centre Workers' Party.

Within the population as a whole black women clearly suffer greatest discrimination and bear the greatest burden. Research shows that 37 per cent of black women are the primary source of their families' income, compared with 12 per cent among white women, and, remarkably, their average monthly income, at about US$50, is only a third of the average income of households headed by white women.

One reason for this is the discrimination black women face on the labour market. Only 9 per cent of black women working outside the home are employed in industry. Whereas 19.6 per sent of white working women are employed as secretaries only 3.9 per cent of black women get white collar jobs. Even though today companies can no longer advertise in newspapers for 'girls of good appearance', which in the past was a coded way of saying white, many black women still find that jobs have mysteriously been filled when they turn up for interviews.

In these circumstances, many black women end up as maids. Domestic service accounts for 56 per cent of the jobs they fill, compared with 24 per cent of the jobs occupied by white women. Others become prostitutes. A popular saying has it that Brazilian prisons are only for the three 'ps' — 'pobres, pardos e putas' ('the poor, blacks and whores'). One could well add that the worst of Brazilian discrimination is reserved for those who fill all three categories simultaneously.

Sue Branford
June 1993

Rural Women

'We've got to get back to our roots'
Dona Rosa, a woman from the Northeast

'My name is Rosa and I'm 54. My dear husband died two years ago, God bless him.

I grew up on the land in Bahia, in the district of Feira de Santana. There were ten of us children at home and from an early age we had to work hard for our keep. That was how it was in those days. My parents were poor peasants, and we lived on what we grew. Not one of us went to school. Only my oldest brother who argued with my father and got thrown out, learned to read and write in the town. I could hardly wait for his monthly visits home. You see, he was teaching me my letters. If the paper he'd brought with him ran out, I used to write them in the sand. That was how I learned my alphabet.

When I was 18 I married my husband. He was 23 years older than me and a widower. We married for love. He brought seven children into the marriage with him, the youngest just 11 months old and the oldest as old as me. That was a heavy burden for me. Only nine months after the wedding my first child was born. It died after six months, of diarrhoea with vomiting. And so it went on. A baby every year. I gave birth twenty times and brought up 14 children. No mother likes to give up her children. I didn't want so many, but I didn't know how to stop them. My husband had no idea, at least we never talked about it. I used to complain and didn't think it was right for men to get their wives pregnant every year. We're poor people and the situation here in Petrolina isn't easy.

At home I lived like a prisoner, with no rights. Just looking after the children, cooking, doing the washing, sweeping up — I never had a second to myself. One day I told my husband that I didn't want to go on living if I wasn't allowed to take part, at least once a week, in the church Bible study group. Because I wasn't — how can

I put it — living at all, neither dead nor alive, just permanently tired and exhausted. After a long battle he gave his permission.

Yes, and then gradually I took part in more and more activities at church. (She laughs).

I took part in everything, because I needed mental and spiritual stimulation. My husband wasn't like that. He only ever thought about how he could feed his family. There wasn't room in his head for anything else. But he was also the only breadwinner, and that was the hardest thing for him. He was a good joiner, used to make furniture, even water canisters for donkeys to carry. But then people didn't pay on time and we were left standing there.

There are days in our family when lunch and the evening meal are one and the same. Then we just eat once in the day and if we don't have anything, we go to bed early, so we don't notice the hunger so much. There are 19 of us now and only three are working. We live out of one saucepan. When we eat, we all eat, when we starve, we all starve. But I tell you in all seriousness, we prefer to starve than not to send the children to school.

I don't want my grown-up daughters to have to work as servants for a family, for starvation wages, from six in the morning until late at night, with no rights, without being allowed to go to school. That's not right. If they want to carry on with school, then they should do that. Yes, they should do that.

When I think back, my whole life has been a struggle against poverty and illness. We all have our crosses to bear. Saying that, I didn't even meet a doctor until after I was married and moved to the town. On the land the only treatment we ever got was with medicinal herbs.

In the town I often had to go to the doctors at the hospital because I was pregnant so often. I lost six children through illness. The doctors didn't do them much good.

The family has had a lot to put up with in the last few years. My son J. used to have terrible nervous attacks, used to threaten us all. He wounded my husband with a knife and ended up in prison, yes, in prison. He should have had psychiatric help. Every day I used to go to the mayor to ask for the money for the bus tickets to Recife (the capital of Pernambuco, about 900km away). The medical insurance was prepared to pay for J. but he needed two attendants to go with him and we didn't have the money. The mayor has funds for things like that, he just doesn't want to dole them out. Only to people who lick his boots. That what it's like here in Petrolina. After 17 days of running to and fro he gave me the money, and J. was able to go into hospital. After 14 days they sent him back. The doctors say his illness can't be cured. Now he has to take strong medication regularly. We all take care. He hasn't had an attack for a year now, but I'm still not happy about it. Every day I pray to God to protect us, because he's the doctor of all doctors and can cure anything.

At the same time my huband was suffering more and more from sclerosis and lost his sight. At night he used to wander around confused and we didn't get any sleep. They were hard times.

When, my son H. suddenly started having epileptic attacks every four months, we almost lost our minds. He has, thank God, been living a very controlled life since then: he's a vegetarian, regularly takes herbal medicines and hasn't had any more attacks. He's a self-confident, disciplined young man and works with me in the herbal medicines centre.

Yes, my work in the herbal medicines centre, I'm glad of it. I tell you quite seriously, that is my mission in life, my calling. I always wanted to give people advice and help them.

Actually, it all began in 1981. We'd set up a church health group locally under the guidance of Sister Maria. It was a First Aid course, only we also went out to people's houses visiting the sick. Sister Maria, who's also a nurse, taught us everything, even how to give injections. Everyone except me learned how to do that, but I didn't have the guts. (She laughs.)

There were 18 of us women and two men doing the course that year. We all hoped to find work later as assistant nurses in the state hospital. In fact, some of them did, not that it did them much good, poor things! The hospital doesn't have any money to treat patients any more. The rooms are empty, there are only three wards left. Anyone who wants treatment there has to take their own drugs with them. There are only a few nurses still working; all the rest were given compulsory leave. Without pay, of course. They'll be paid at some time in the future.

But I wanted to tell you how our herbal medicine centre came about. In 1981 the theme of the Church's community-based campaign was "health for all". We each got a pamphlet about it which we worked through in the Bible study group and with Sister Maria on the health course. The pamphlet suggested that we should go back to herbal medicines. Most of the women didn't have a clue about medicinal herbs, although they didn't like having to run to the doctor with every little illness. And who has the money to buy medicine anyway? So we cottoned on very quickly that it would be useful for us women if we could go back to our household remedies. After all, as mothers we bear total responsibility for our families, don't we? We're the ones who have to go running to the doctor if someone gets ill. We're the ones who have to wait there for hours on end. And then we have to juggle with our husbands' starvation wages to buy the medicine. I won't go on about how everything else which happens in the home is our responsibility too. Even bringing up the children is our job.

Anyway, we thought it was a good suggestion and started to gather plants and study their properties. Because we wanted to put on an exhibition about it all, we stuck them onto pieces of card and drew diagrams of them. There had to be detailed descriptions of where the plants grew, when they could be picked and how they should be prepared. Each of us had to concentrate on a particular ailment.

It was a big job, and we worked on it for weeks and put a lot of love and care into it. Each of us was supposed to learn which plants were good for which ailments. I still remember how difficult it was for me at the beginning, but in the end it wasn't so difficult after all and I stuck everything on and finished it all properly. After that I felt a bit more "developed". (She laughs.)

And then, after our plant exhibition, which was really good, we carried on gathering plants, and I started a small plant pharmacy. At some point I also started to cultivate a small herb garden behind the church. That was heavy work, because the ground here is very hard and stony. It needs a lot of fertiliser and water. Every morning I had to get up at four o' clock to water the plants. That was the only time of day that you could get a trickle of water from the mains. I dug circular beds with little walls around them so that the precious water wouldn't flow away. Even the trees and bushes were watered because they provided shade. The sun here in the Northeast scorches everything. It was hard work, but sometimes my children helped me.

Celerino, the famous plant doctor, came here a few times, and he taught us a lot. Once I was even able to go to Pesqueira to see him and attend a weekend seminar. There I met some women from right up in the Northeast, who were also starting herb gardens in their communities. It was fantastic talking to them and swapping experiences. Unfortunately, my old man wasn't keen on me working outside Petrolina, so I never went back. That's the way it is. Anyway, I ran the herb garden and the plant pharmacy on my own for four years, when the sisters weren't there. I gave advice and sold the herbs for very little. I also gave cuttings to anyone who wanted them.

Now that the sisters are back, we also treat people with herbs, mud and vegetarian diets. We get a lot of patients from up-country. It doesn't matter what's wrong with them, we don't turn anyone away. Most people stay here for four or five days and learn how to treat their ailments. Then they carry on treating themselves at home with the same remedies. The people who have money pay, the people who don't are treated free. I can tell whether someone's really poor from their eyes. We know poverty ourselves and can recognise it in others. We basically survive on donations, because more poor people come here than rich ones. But people who are healed like to give something. Sometimes things are touch and go here because we're so short of money. After all, salaries have to be paid to eight women and four young people — and then there's the other costs.

So far God has always helped us to carry on. I just work in the pharmacy now because I had an accident and can't lift heavy weights any more. I make up teas, syrups, ointments and creams myself, sort the plants, dry and sell them and give advice. If the nurse isn't there, I stand in for her. She taught me how to diagnose a person's illness from their eyes.

The other women work in the garden, in the kitchen or with the patients and the young people help them. But between you and me, most of them don't have the right attitude. It seems to me that they're being inconsistent when they tell the patients that plants and a diet of raw vegetarian food are heathy, then before the patients' very eyes, eat unhealthy things like biscuits and sweets themselves. I've already told the sisters they should find women who can be trained and given some responsibility. Here everybody's always shouting for Rosa, Rosa and thinks that I do all right on my own. But that's no good. When I die there has to be someone here to take over from me, people who have the right attitude and will carry on my work. I've told the sisters that.

You asked whether I'm happy in my work? I tell you, seriously, I feel fulfilled. And I thank God for giving me an open mind where nature is concerned. It's all there for our health and well-being. That was really an important discovery for me.'

Recorded by Helga Oberländer

Women farmworkers in the Northeast

In one state in the Northeast of Brazil women farmworkers have joined together to form a broad movement to fight for their rights. Their organisation is called the Women Farmworkers' Movement, (MMT). This chapter explores its history, methods and politics.

One of the region's most serious problems is that here, as elsewhere in Brazil, the land is concentrated in a few hands. The bulk of the fertile land is left by the big landowners to lie fallow. If it is used at all, it is for plantations of sugar-cane or pineapples, or as grazing for cattle.

Small parcels of land on these estates are cultivated by tenant families under the most difficult conditions. More and more of them are being driven out, and most cannot defend their right of use. According to the law, families which have worked a plot of land for at least one year cannot be driven from that land. However, the power of the big landowner is undiminished; the judiciary and the police are generally open to bribery. Hence the people live in desperate poverty right in the middle of fertile land.

The MMT was born at the beginning of the 1980s, towards the end of the military dictatorship, out of the work of the Catholic Church's land rights support group (CPT). Under the dictatorship the Church was the only outlet for social protest.

At that time a great many farmworkers regularly attended CPT meetings in the district town, but only three of them were women. It annoyed these women that the men had the chance to learn about Brazil's political situation while their wives had to stay at home, so they decided to organise a meeting exclusively for women farmworkers. It meant a great deal of work; in a region covering 200 square kilometers, they went from house to house in the villages and hamlets inviting women to the meeting.

It was hugely successful, with fifty women attending. They talked together about their lives and described, in words and pictures, their major problems. Four main issues emerged:

— landlessness
— the unjust wages paid to women day labourers
— machismo
— poor health

At the next meeting, two months later, the women drew up a programme of action. They organised meetings in the various villages and called bimonthly central meetings. They also elected a ten woman co-ordinating committee, which meets monthly.

Later the MMT broke away from the CPT. It also retains its independence from the unions and political parties, although the women do work closely with the Brazilian Central Workers' Organisation (CUT) and the Workers' Party (PT).

Today the MMT touches the lives of around 7,000 women throughout the region. These women have formed small village groups which meet regularly. In a search for financial independence, women in some of the villages have formed production groups selling jointly produced bread, confectionery and needlework. The profits go into setting up new groups. At a local level the women are organised by occupation: washerwomen, day labourers, farmworkers, domestic servants and teachers employed by the local councils (*municípios*). Women teachers in rural areas have often only attended primary school themselves. Some earn just a tenth of the national minimum wage. Each occupational group meets to work on its own specific needs and rights — for example, at one meeting, women farmworkers discussed alternative farming techniques.

The women consider spreading information about healthcare to be one of their most important tasks. They hold weekend workshops on various themes (the female body, contraception, pregnancy, children, illnesses, nutrition) and give the women the opportunity to swap traditional remedies and learn about new ones under the guidance of a nurse. The women then take this knowledge back to their local groups.

Often the women get into trouble at home for working in the MMT. For this reason they invite their husbands to 'spouses weekends' at which the men's own behaviour is portrayed in role-play and then discussed.

Every year there is a state-wide meeting at which the women discuss and evaluate the past year's work and develop plans for the coming year.

The MMT aims to give women the opportunity to escape the isolation of their own homes, to become politically aware and to take part in the political struggle. The results in the region are already clearly visible: more and more women are standing as candidates in local and trade union elections. Songs written by MMT women are heard everywhere and play an important part in raising awareness.

One fundamental part of the MMT's work is its participation in the struggle for agrarian reform, the lack of which is seen as the main cause of exploitation and oppression.

As a women's organisation, the MMT sees itself as part of the workers' class struggle. 'We must participate together in the struggles', says one of the MMT's introductory leaflets. 'Men and women must take part as equals in changing society. But if this equality is to be effective, then women must not only eliminate discrimination at work and in the unions, but also discrimination in the family and in their relationships with men.'

Christiane Fröhlich and Dorothea Hillingshäuser

'I've suffered, but I've won through'
Maria's Story

'I come from the country
from up-country
listen to me
I'm a Brazilian woman
a worker
and I live in pain'

Maria Aparecida's story comes from her own writings and from a song she composed for a rally held to mark International Women's day.

'I learnt early on what suffering meant. My father thought that women and girls were nothing. He used to say *"Mulher não é gente"* (Women aren't people).

At home I was locked up. I wasn't allowed to have friends either, not even woman friends, and I was often beaten. I hated having been born a girl and envied my brothers like crazy.

Then there was the poverty. We often went hungry. My father had to sell our little plot of land, so we were tenants on a big landowner's *fazenda* (estate). Half of the harvest had to be handed over to the owner as rent. What was left wasn't enough for all of us. Two of the children didn't survive. Hunger and death are everyday occurrences for most of the families in our area.

I thought school was great fun, but after four years my father stopped me going any more. Sending girls to school was like casting pearls before swine, he said.

At 16 I thought I could escape from my father by getting married, so I married the first man who came along. But what I'd let myself in for was worse than I could ever have imagined. It was hell. You see, my husband was an oppressor too. He made me the slave he'd always wanted. I had one child after another, and I was either shut up at home with the babies or had to slog out in the fields.

I had my children, who I had to feed, on one side and a husband who only gave orders on the other. How I suffered!

The worst thing was when he used to hit the children and I wasn't allowed to intervene. He never once hit me, but the endless mental beatings that I had were far harder. If ever I wanted to cry on my mother's shoulder, she used to say, "Take it easy, daughter, don't get worked up about it. Women are born to suffer. And they have to obey their husbands — *mulher não é gente!"*

I lived in this hell for ten years. My life seemed to get more pointless every day. I used to get very ill. I'd lie on the bed for days on end and cry, with the children bawling around me.

Finally I reached the end of my tether and wrote to a doctor who used to give advice on a local radio station. He replied, saying that I was neither physically ill nor crazy. All I had to do was change my life. Easy for him to say that! I made a mental note of it, but couldn't see any way out. Then, a short time later I took the first step after all. Our parish had begun to organise itself into a base Christian community. Men and women got together at meetings regularly. My husband let me go because it was the Church. It would have been hard for him to ban that. At last I could talk to other people. We talked about our lives. Glimmers of hope. But there wasn't much we could change at that point.

Soon after that we were visited by three women, farmworkers like me. We talked about my life, about the women who lived in the interior and then the three of them invited me to the town. A meeting of the Church's land rights support group (CPT) was going to be held there two months later, and only women were invited. I knew straight away I had to go, whatever it took. Naturally, my husband said I couldn't. Me alone in the town, away from home for a whole day! He couldn't imagine it. I fought, he was furious, but whenever he was exhausted I started to work on him again. That lasted two months and finally, on the evening before the meeting, I got his permission to go. That moment changed my life and my family's for ever.

That first women's meeting was followed by others. Together we learned to recognise our worth as women. And we realised how important it was that women organise, because no one can change anything alone!

At the meetings, we recognised that we were oppressed, and that society lives by exploiting us. We're fighting against that now. We know our rights.

Actually, this whole struggle started at home. From talking to the other women, I realised that my husband had a massive inferiority complex because he was illiterate. It was tough, but I managed to persuade him to do a literacy course. They not only taught him to read and write, but also something about the situation and the rights of the workers. He calmed down, stopped hitting the children, and later also accepted my going to the many women's meetings. At one point he even admitted having done a lot of things that he shouldn't have done. Today he fights alongside me in the union.

In 1986, together with 39 other families, we occupied a *fazenda*. Ten of these families had been tenants on this land for years. Then suddenly the owner doubled the rent and said we now had to pay in advance, instead of at the end of the year. We couldn't, and for all of us it would have meant having to move to some town *favela*. But there were a couple of us women who, through our meetings, knew our rights as tenants. We organised our families, mobilised other families and occupied the land. Together we built huts and began to plant the various bits of land on the *fazenda* which had lain fallow for ages. The owner hired hit men and threatened us, saying he'd destroy our harvest with tractors. Later the courts awarded us the land. The former owner appealed, and the case has been dragging on ever since. We're still getting death threats, but we're not giving in. If men and women fight together against exploitation, then we'll change society!

Today women in our region are organised in the Women Farmworkers' Movement, (MMT). I work for it as a co-ordinator, and a women's group meets regularly in our village. Not long ago I was elected president of the farmworkers' union in our district. I'm also active in the Church. I want to persuade lots more women to emancipate themselves and their families so that together we can fight for a free and just future.'

'*Companheira*, come with me,
for this battle is also your battle.'

Recorded by Christiane Fröhlich and Dorothea Hillingshäuser

Oysters, shrimps, crabs
The world of fisherwomen

It is December 1989 in a fishing village on Brazil's Northeast coast, a coast much praised in tourist brochures. A young girl, the daughter of a fisherwoman, passes a rubbish dump on her way to school. Since her breakfast — as so often — has not satisfied her, the girl scavenges for something more to eat among the rubbish. She comes across a large piece of something which looks like meat. As she burrows deeper, she hears a whimper. She finds a baby; it is still alive. She digs the baby out of the rubbish, picks it up and takes it home to her mother. Her mother, who cannot even fill the bellies of her own children, is so horrified at the baby's plight that she takes it into her own family with the words, 'You've brought us the baby Jesus'.

The fisherwomen in this town meet regularly. At Christmas this year, which they celebrate together, the foundling is at the centre of events. During the Christmas festival they stand silently for a long while around the child lying in their midst. Finally one fisherwoman breaks the perplexed silence, proclaiming, 'The child is God's sign that he is with us in our fight.'

Constant worry about their families' survival is just one aspect of the fisherwomen's struggle. Some of the women are also involved, with the fishermen, in the political battle to defend their way of life.

Fishing off the coast in the rivers and the artificial lakes has provided a living for many families for generations. Today around ten million people still earn a livelihood directly from fishing. Only a small fraction of them (around 20,000 — those who work for the large companies) use industrial methods. The rest work in the traditional way, using the methods employed by their forefathers for generations. Their equipment includes flat-bottomed boats, small nets, fish traps, lines and simple rods. Large numbers live, like their forefathers, in shabby mud huts with a floor space of twenty to forty square metres, many without mains water supply, electricity or sanitation.

The working and living conditions of fishing families have always been hard, but for the fisherwomen the situation is doubly difficult because many men drink away their earnings. They leave their wives to provide for their families alone even though the women generally earn less than their husbands.

Among traditional fishing families a sexual division of labour has evolved. The majority of the men go out onto the high seas in small boats for a week or so at a time. The women, on the other hand, travel to the mangrove swamps near the coast each day. Travelling can take up to two hours, and their working hours are dependent on water levels. They set off for the fishing grounds somewhere between four and eight in the morning, depending on the tides. Normally five to seven women travel together at ebb-tide and stay for around six hours.

The majority search for oysters, mussels and shrimps; often they spend hours bent double in the mud under the mangrove trees in blinding sunshine or in wind and rain. Others catch large crabs from their boats with simple baited lines. If they are lucky, they may take one or even two kilos of fish and seafood home with them. Although most of the women travel to work in groups, the yield is not shared. If the boat they use is not their own, then they have to hand over part of their catch to the owner; the rest is theirs.

The vast majority of the fishing families have no land of their own on which to cultivate basic foodstuffs like cassava and beans. The women therefore must sell part of their catch. In this way they become totally dependent on middle-men who buy cheaply and then sell at double the price.

Some of the traders only accept the flesh of the shellfish. Since most of the fisherwomen have no fridge in which to keep shellfish, they are broken open immediately after being caught. The children have to help. In a good month, the women earn the equivalent of a minimum wage, but their income depends on the size of their catch and there are days when there is no money at all and the family goes hungry.

When the women come home from this strenuous work, they have to do the housework, the washing, the cleaning and so on. In many fishing villages there are still no day nurseries, so the fisherwomen must rely on grandparents or neighbours to look after their children while they are at work. Most fisherwomen are illiterate but their daughters are able to attend school, although there is generally no money for school materials. Boys have to accompany their fathers from the age of ten to learn how to fish.

The already harsh working conditions endured by fishing families have deteriorated due to increasing water pollution and land speculation. As the tourist industry expands in the Northeast of Brazil, the coastal regions are becoming increasingly attractive to land speculators. Hotels and holiday villas are springing up everywhere. The fishing families, who have always lived and stored their fishing equipment on the coast, are gradually being forced inland. Out of ignorance most of them have not legally registered the plot of land on which they have lived for generations. Speculators are now shrewdly appropriating such land for themselves.

If a large landowner buys a forest, the women are often no longer allowed to continue gathering shellfish there. In order to survive, some of the women have to fish secretly in such areas, running the gauntlet of mounted guards hired by the landowners. When pursued, they hide in the forests and give each other courage by praying together. The development of the coasts will undoubtedly destroy the mangrove forests on which the fisherwomen rely. Brazil's increased water pollution stems from a programme devised by the military regime during the 1970s; in order to reduce the country's reliance on oil from the outside world, Brazil's car engines were converted to consume alcohol produced from home-grown sugar-cane. Since then the highly profitable cane fields have spread coastwards in Pernambuco, Paraíba and Alagoas. The number of factories which distil sugar into alcohol is increasing at a similar rate, and the waste waters produced during the distillation process are pumped into the rivers. Paper mills and the chemical industry also rank among the worst water polluters. Some of Brazil's rivers are so contaminated that fishing is no longer possible.

At a meeting in 1985 aimed at getting the fishing community's demands incorporated into the new constitution one fisherwoman spoke out: 'Companheiras who, like me, live from fishing, only ever catch waste to eat these days. We have companheiras with 10 or 15 children who've had to build their houses right in the middle of the rubbish. They go to work with their children only to catch a sack full of rubbish. Rosinha, a mother of eight, already has maxixe, a skin disease, which causes acute leg pains. We have to put a stop to water pollution.'

The poisoning of the rivers has cut the fisherwomen's catch dramatically. Their incomes are often no longer enough to feed whole families. On bad days some of the fisherwomen do without food so that their children can eat. They eat mud to deaden the hunger and then try their luck again the next day in the same dirty water.

Nor is it only the women's livelihood which is being destroyed in this environmental disaster; ever worsening water pollution is also damaging their already poor state of health. Previously the causes of their illnesses could be traced back to their working practices, unhygienic living conditions and bad diet. Typical ailments include rheumatism, pains in the spinal column, influenza, inflammation of the lungs and leg injuries. Because the women spend hours standing in damp mud and brackish water, generally bent double, their spines and knees are put under serious strain. The alternation between dampness, warmth and wind triggers regular chills which can lead to inflammation of the lungs, and the mud in which the women wade is full of sharp shellfish with the result that they often injure themselves. The contaminated mud then makes it more difficult for wounds to heal, often leading to phlebitis.

The poisoned mud also causes serious skin diseases and inflammation of the pelvic organs. While fishing the women sometimes sink down into the mud and find themselves up to their hips in muddy water.

In the past it was usual for women to have a break from work for a few days during their periods or after the birth of a child. Traditional rules protect fisherwomen from the evil spirits by prohibiting them from washing their hair or eating certain fruits during this time. However these days pollution-reduced catches mean that the women can no longer observe traditional laws of this kind. One fisherwoman told how the contaminated mud had caused a friend to have periods lasting 15 days. Unless she went to work she had no money to feed her many children.

Fishing families who refuse to put up with their lot have been organising for several years in various locations along the coast and on the rivers and artificial lakes. From 1920 until 1988 they were forced by the state to join *colônias* — trade union federations — in order to keep their fishing rights. These *colônias* were controlled by the navy, and the interests of the state inevitably came before those of fishing families.

In a bid to break free, some communities began to meet with nuns and priests under the auspices of the Church's fishing support groups, founded in Olinda in 1968. They worked together to develop an independent and democratic organisation, to oppose land speculation and the pollution of the environment, and to improve the social support system available to fishermen and women.

It was fisherwomen who first went public in the struggle for social welfare, condemning the miserable conditions in which they were compelled to live and work. With their efforts, the 1988 constitution contained a provision stating that self-employed fishermen and women were entitled to claim free state health care; for the women that means that they can give birth in state hospitals. The new constitution also entitles fisherwomen to draw a pension if they are 55 years of age or have been working for 25 years — and can prove it, which is often difficult.

The fisherwomen had to fight hard for the right to take part in this process, since most men believe that women should not become involved in politics. It was only a few years ago that women were even allowed to join the *colônias*, since the men threatened to leave if women were granted membership.

In some places nuns working with the fishing support groups began to invite fisherwomen to regular, separate meetings. One such group of fisherwomen in a town north of Recife have now been meeting once a week for ten years. The task is daunting, since the women are always exhausted after the long day's work, but in the autumn of 1989 the nuns' efforts culminated in the women compiling their own slate of candidates for the local *colônia's* presidential electlons. They emerged victorious. Joana, the first woman president to be elected by a *colônia* anywhere in Brazil, is referred to somewhat sneeringly by her male colleagues as the *presidente de saia*, 'the beskirted president'. She and the other two women on the management committee will find it difficult to counter the fishermen's prejudices. To what extent the new woman president will be able to gain acceptance for the specific demands of the women in her *colônia* remains to be seen.

Gerborg Meister

Urban Women

An everyday story
Life in a *favela*

'My mother came from the North. One day my father left to go to Rio to look for work. Not once did he send us any money. At the time my mother was pregnant with me. She just sold everything and moved to Rio with eleven children. It took her twenty years to find him — in the end she did it through a missing person's appeal on the radio. He'd had an accident on a building site where he was working and had been crippled.

I was born and grew up in the *favela*. When I was little you could climb trees and play catch there, but that's not possible any more. There are too many huts now and no empty spaces, and these days the police regularly turn up, start shooting and cart people off at random.

Not long ago my youngest came running back and said that the police were beating up his brother. He is 16 and was on his way to the bakery where he works. I just dropped everything. I searched for my son for days, going from one youth welfare office to another. After eight days he turned up in the youth police detention centre. He'd been beaten black and blue. Where had he been all this time? And why? No one told me. But I know that the reason they mistreated my son was to extract information about so-called criminals up here.

At the age of 13 I was still a child but no longer a virgin. They forced me into it, by beating me and threatening me. I wasn't even 15 when my first child, a boy, was born. He died at three months. He used to cry a lot, so I took him to the doctor. The doctor didn't undress him, didn't examine him at all. He just gave me some medicine, which I gave to my baby. The first time he stopped crying immediately. So I carried on, like the doctor had said. On the third time, he died. Then my sister read the instructions — it was for cramps, for adults. Later we found out that my baby had had a serious ear infection. I wanted to press charges against the doctor, but then I thought: that won't bring the child back. After all, they always have more clout than we do. If the baby died, then it was God's will. Otherwise someone would have read the instructions sooner.

I used to have a small hut right down by the mountainside. We used to worry whenever it rained, wondering what we'd do if the roof didn't hold. Then the hut began to collapse, so the fire brigade came and took it down. After that I found a new place. That was two years ago now, and I still haven't finished sorting it out. How can I? I do everything on my own, with the children. I earn very little. I used to sew at home for a factory, but then the sewing machine packed up and I didn't have any money to get it fixed. Where would I have got it from? I had no other choice but to look for work as a cleaner. So I climb up high and clean open windows from the outside. I'm terrified the whole time that I might fall, but I have to do it.

I have been on the game and I've begged. I thank God that I'm out of that, but I'll never forget it. My greatest wish is to get a bit of money together to do up my hut, so that this one doesn't fall apart too. I don't ask for any more than that. My hut is all lop-sided and crooked and it leaks like mad, but to me it's a palace. After all, that's where I'm raising my kids.

Mind you, I've enjoyed life too. The best time was when I was out and about with my first husband. I used to go dancing, had friends, used to go to parties. But now I've got my children. I look after them the best I can. I won't leave them in the lurch and I'm not giving them away.

Their fathers? There are always plenty of men willing to make children, but when it comes to finding one to raise them you have to look long and hard. That's why I get rid of them if I can. I've done that many a time. Once after an abortion I ended up in hospital for four months. I'd a pierced womb and it was touch and go whether I'd live.

I really have to get rid of them. Now it's a bit easier, of course. I can help myself, get rid of them myself. When the time comes I don't call anyone. God forgive me, but I had no choice. I didn't have money to buy contraceptives; what little I had wasn't even enough for the basics. Then all of a sudden there was the coil. But even with the coil I still got pregnant. The girl's 15 now.

I lost my last baby six years ago. After that the doctor where I was working tied my fallopian tubes for me and it stopped. I've often prayed to God for forgiveness, he knows why I did it. But he'll never forgive *that* sin, though I believe he understands. I love my children very much though I've already forgotten their fathers.

City people are very prejudiced against us here in the *favela*. But there are good and bad people everywhere, here among us and among them too. I have worked a lot for rich people. I know what they're like. How many sons of rich parents are there who intentionally run people over with their cars, kill people and lots more besides? The poor don't steal on a large scale. The rich have money and use it to get everything hushed up. The poor have nothing, they steal to survive.

The worst thing is this poverty. As soon as you get a few more pennies in your pocket everything gets more expensive again, the bus, cooking oil, everything. One day all hell's going to break loose; you can't put up indefinitely with seeing children go hungry, or fine ladies pushing their fully-laden trolleys to the cash desk when you've got as good as nothing in your hands. I'd like just once to meet the rich man who could manage on my wage. He'd have to eat beans and cassava flour, like I do.

Living here's not easy. You get so tired. Your legs get covered in varicose veins, up and down the mountain on foot every day. We have to lug water and everything up here and the paths are lousy.

Of course we want a better life. All of us here want that, but how? There's no shortage of co-operation. Neighbours and friends all help each other. But even with the help of others, you can only build a brick house if you have the money. For me it's impossible. What I earn doesn't even fill our stomachs. All I have is my two arms and God. I don't care which god, the one the Catholics worship, the Pentecostalists' god or the *Macumba* god. As I see it, there's just one god for everyone. The Church used to be there just for praying. Today I can see that it's fighting with us: for the rights of the people in the *favelas*, the domestics, the workers. All I only know is that my faith is very strong. And that gives me strength and life.'

Bibliography

Frances O'Gorman, 'Mulheres da Rocinha e da St. Marta', in *Morro, Mulher*, Ed. Paulinas e Fase-Programa Nuclar; 1984

Anna Lúcia Florisbela dos Santos

The Washerwoman

This woman...
Simple. Serene. Self-forgetting...
Her weary arms
rest on her knees...
She stares vacantly ahead
Lost in her world
of bundles and lather —
the washerwoman.

Raw, deformed hands.
Wet washing.
Short fingers.
Cracked nails.
Corns.
Painfully scarred.
On her wedding finger a cheap ring of
metal. Remembrance.

An expression of forlornness,
time stands still.
Around her —
a cloud of white suds.

The day has not yet begun
in the house of Our Lord God.
The first washing line
hails the rising sun,
the laundry transforms colour,
becomes bright, multi-coloured.
This woman,
forty washed-out years,
twelve children,
grown-up and growing.

A widow, of course.
Composed, dutiful, plucky.
She fears the punishment of Heaven.
Curled up in her poor world.

She rises early.
Greets the red sky,

waits for the sun.
Opens the doors of the day
between bundles and troughs.

Silently dreaming.
The children are growing,
her heavy hands work.

The limits of her world,
the laundry, the meadow.
Lines and pegs.
The washtub.
In the evenings — the iron.

She washes and struggles and lives
and raises twelve children.
Who are slowly growing.
Curled up in her poor world,
in a cloud of
white suds.

I dedicate this short poem,
to the washerwomen of my home,
on the Rio Vermelho,
with deep respect.

Cora Coralina

Source: *Poemas dos Becos de Goiás e Estórias Mais* (Poems from Goiás and Other Tales), Cora Coralina, Global Editora, São Paulo, 1988, p.207

Explosive Chemistry
Organising women in factories

'My name is... well, the name's not important. I'm a worker. I come from São Paulo, and my parents came from up-country. From there they moved to this town, which to them was always the "city", the "industrial town", the "city of progress". They allowed themselves to be hoodwinked by the propaganda put out by the military dictatorship, which convinced them life would be better in the city. It was a rude awakening; it was very hard for us, because we'd given up our little plot of land, which at least fed us.

With nowhere to live, no money and no hope of going back, we all had to get on and earn something. I was the oldest and therefore the first to go out to work.

I worked in a detergent factory and the little I earned was at least a help at home, even if my wages were very low; I was a minor and had no legal protection. To me it seemed a lot, and I was happy to earn even half the minimum wage to help my father pay the rent. At the time I had no idea just how much we were being exploited. There were five of us at home and originally only my father worked. Then I started work and the two of us kept the family. But as time went on our money was worth less and less, and my wages no longer covered the rent.

I worked on the factory floor, and although I was legally under age, I worked an eight-hour day, or longer. Apparently the head of department liked my work. I took part in everything — it was all new to me. I was pretty enthusiastic too, curious, asked a lot of questions. I think that was why he noticed me. I liked the department and learned all there was to learn. My relationship with the boss was good. I think I must have been very naive, but I had the same kind of relationship with the boss as with the other people in the department.

Some of my colleagues thought I was always sucking up to him, but I didn't notice. I didn't have any ulterior motive. When they took on some new people, some of them from other factories, people who were already more experienced. Among them were some very nice girls who taught me to think differently. I realised that they had a different relationship with the management. They were harassed, for example, they weren't allowed to leave their seats. That wasn't fair, because in that company we were actually allowed to go off and get materials whenever we needed them. Anyhow, I owe it to my colleagues that I developed somewhat.

The Church also made me more aware of the exploitation to which I and my female colleagues were being subjected. My family are very devout Catholics, and the only place that my father used to let us go was to church. But our parish was pretty progressive, and it was there that I heard for the first time of God as the liberator of the poor, of Jesus amongst the poor, of how the Church was on the side of the poor. Our parish even supported striking industrial workers in the region.

I started to think about all that, but also about my church's attitudes, and I realised that I was being exploited on three different levels — as a woman, as a minor and as a poor person. I knew then that I had to do something. So I started to attend my female colleagues' meetings at the factory and realised how many problems they had, mainly because they were married and had children. At one meeting someone asked which of us were going to school or doing vocational training, and I was the only one. After all, I still lived at home and was single. One colleague explained her problems:

"You finish work and you're tired, because after all it wears you down physically ... and also emotionally, because of the bosses. And then you still have to get home. I, for example, have to catch four buses to get to work. School? How? First work and then school till eleven at night, you're never home before half twelve, and then you have to get up again at half five the next day to go off again, and more than likely you fall asleep at work. I don't have the stomach for it. And then there's also the chance that you might be attacked."

We discussed lots of different problems of that kind, and what shocked us most was that many of our colleagues who had done vocational training had never received a job contract commensurate with their qualifications. Vocational training? That was for men.

I worked in that factory for five years and by the end I was very active on the workers' committee. Once I even represented the workers on a wage negotiating committee. We went on strike for 16 days and forced them to accept our demands. But a week after the strike ended all the workers on the committee were dismissed, including me. It was very sad, because we were a strong and well-organised group. But, the battle had to go on. After all, my family still needed my help, although by then my sisters were earning too.

I got a new job in another chemical factory, once again on the factory floor. There I was elected onto the works' committee by my colleagues. At that time I was really developing politically, through my trade union work and through the Church's Workers' Support Group, a church institution which concerns itself with the workers' living and working conditions — and which works with them so that they become aware of how they are being exploited.

As a member of the works' committee, I was able to see my female colleagues' problems at first hand. There were lots of things that used to depress me, and one event that really shocked me. We all used to bring our lunch to work with us in canteens which were placed in a large water bath an hour before lunch time. On one occasion there was a group of social workers in the factory; they were doing a study of the living conditions of the working class. Without the knowledge of the other women, the company management allowed the social workers to open some of the canteens so that they could find out what the workers ate. It was a real shock; many of the containers were empty, others contained just a piece of bread. Some of my colleagues obviously used to leave their canteens to warm up simply because they were ashamed to admit to the others that they had nothing to eat. If a canteen was empty, it was fair to assume that there wasn't anything at home for the children either.

I realised then that neither companies nor the government had any interest in creating the conditions which would make the workers' lives fit for human beings. All they want is to carry on getting richer.

I don't work in a factory any more, but for the Church's Workers' Support Group as an educator. I organise groups which help people to reflect on their own lives through their faith and the Bible. I can't carry on with school or study at the moment; I just can't afford it, but the dream is still there... of life, of something to smile about, of the struggle, of love... Perhaps tomorrow, who knows?

When I'm not working or at school, in the evenings, I'm constantly fighting, not only for fair wages, but for our work to be recognised and for decent working conditions for my fellow women workers, many who feed their families single-handed, and finally for companies and the government to observe the laws of the land.'

Recorded by Cecília Camargo

Made with fear

On 15 July 1989 the women working at the De Millus lingerie factory in Rio de Janeiro went on strike. Their action triggered a far-reaching campaign exposing the working conditions for women and girls. The majority of the strikers were young women under the age of 18, their slogan, 'De Millus, made with fear — boycott this brand!'

No one who passes the factory and reads the huge advertising slogan, 'De Millus is made with love', could imagine that behind these walls there lurks a cynical, misanthropic system. In this factory the new constitution's pronouncements on the rights of women and women workers are not worth the paper they are written on.

The factory employs 3,000 staff (95 per cent women), of which the majority is 14 to 16 years old. The young women there work an eight-hour-day or longer. They get no extra money and no overtime pay. Minors are taken in the main as apprentices and as such are paid less than the minimum wage. By law, under-age apprentices do not have to be paid a full wage, but are not allowed to work an eight-hour-day. However, at De Millus under-age women workers are paid the reduced wage for a working day which exceeds eight hours.

The agreed basic wage is paid only to workers who reach the production target set by the factory management. However, reaching their target requires more than eight hours' work. Moreover, if a worker reaches the target on 29 days of the month, but fails on the thirtieth she does not receive her basic wage. In this factory there is no extra pay for extra work, instead extra work is a prerequisite for workers receiving the wages which they are guaranteed by law.

Every failure to reach the production targets elicits a warning: three warnings are 'reasonable grounds' for dismissal. (This practice guarantees the company a high staff turnover and saves it social welfare costs.)

In an attempt to reach the production target, the women who work in the factory only go to the toilet once a day and restrict themselves to a 20-minute lunch break. Consequently, bladder complaints are commonplace. During menstruation the situation is considerably worse. Female job applicants are also forced to undergo pregnancy tests before the company will employ them, and annual tests of this kinds are compulsory for under-age women workers.

'The product doesn't benefit the producer', that is the logic of capitalism, and it is fully applied by De Millus. Female workers are prohibited from wearing any item of underwear produced by the firm. If they do, they are immediately suspected of theft. Body searches are conducted daily in a cubicle which has no doors or curtains.

Marilena de Almeida Silva was dismissed, along with 300 colleagues, for being a member of the strike committee. She recalls, 'We had to put up with daily searches. It was really humiliating. We had to strip down to our knickers, and when we were having a period, we had to show the tip of the sanitary towel so that they could see that we hadn't hidden anything.'

Many of the women workers are forced to model items of underwear (bras and briefs) produced by the company — without pay, of course. In return they are often molested during fittings, but are neither allowed to complain nor to refuse to take part.

One indignant woman gave the following description of conditions in the factory: 'They don't treat us like human beings here, we don't have time to eat properly and we go to the toilet once, at most twice a day. That's the only way we can earn the basic wage. We work like madmen, and at the end of the month our money is hardly enough to buy two of the hundreds of bras that we've made.'

The strikers were demanding a 100 per cent cost-of-living wage rise, an end to compulsory body searches, paid overtime, the payment of the basic wage prescribed by law and the abolition of dismissal on 'reasonable grounds'.

De Millus is a prime example of how the capitalist exploitation to which all women workers in Brazil are exposed is intensified by machismo.

Cecilia Camargo

On the move
Isabel's story

Asked 'What is your greatest dream', many people from the Northeast of Brazil say that one day they would like to go to São Paulo to find work and for once to earn enough money to live like human beings.

Droughts, the unjust distribution of land in Brazil, an acute lack of job and training opportunities and miserable wages are some of the social reasons why many people seek alternative means of survival.

According to estimates, around a quarter of all Brazilians move from one region to another at some time during their lives. But for many the dream of a better life ends in a big-city slum.

It is difficult to say what proportion of these migrants is female. The majority are young people who have left their homes in the hope of changing their lives. Sometimes they take their families with them, but often older people and women stay behind. This is the only possible explanation for the obvious surplus of women in some regions. Many of these women have difficulty in finding partners. They are never able to fulfil their desire to become wives and mothers and are forced to fill their lives with other things. They too may have to leave their homes.

Isabel tells of her fight for her education.

'My name's Isabel. I was born in 1946 in a small country town in the state of Ceará in the Northeast of Brazil, the sixth child in our family. My mother was very ill when I was born, so she couldn't look after me, and my uncle, who already had nine children of his own, took me in. We lived in the next village, so I didn't have daily contact with my parents and my brothers and sisters. But because of the family ties I never lost touch with them.

I spent my childhood and youth sheltered in the bosom of my family. Because of the school situation in our village, I was only able to attend the *primaria* (which at the time was officially four school years). In my free time I used to help my uncle in the fields.

When I was 22, there was a big row in our family. I was still living with my parents, since I hadn't yet found anyone to marry. But my brother José had a girlfriend. My parents didn't accept her at all, because she came — like my family — from humble origins. My parents wanted something better for us children. So they didn't approve of the relationship. But as my brother and his girlfriend were very, very fond of each other, I took their side in the quarrel. In order to sort the problem out, they married against my parents' wishes. Of course, they couldn't stay in our village after the wedding.

They decided to go to the state of Pará, where three of my other brothers were already working. Because of the rumpus with my parents, I couldn't stay there any more either. So I tagged along witn my brother José and his wife. I cherished the secret hope that I would be able to continue with my education in Pará.

José was lucky enough to find work farming a plot of land for a big landowner. For a while I stayed to help him, but there wasn't a school there for me. So I was forced to move to the nearest town. I wanted an education and that was the only way to get one. Once there, I had to look for a family who needed a maid during the day, but who would give me time off to go to school in the evenings. It wasn't altogether easy.

During the two years I spent in Pará I worked for three different families and put up with a lot so that I could go to school. The first family was a family of 13, only two of them women. There was always masses of work to do, since the men used to leave all sorts of filth around the place. They didn't lift a finger. Everything was left for me. I had to get up as early as half past five to tidy up the living room, do the shopping and cook the meal. Then there were always huge piles of clothes to be washed. The hours weren't fixed, so I couldn't go to school until I'd done all my work for the day. As a result, I often got to school late and missed part of the lesson. All I was paid was my food and free accommodation. At first that was very important to me, because after all I didn't have anything at all when I arrived. But I needed money for school. I had to buy myself exercise books and pencils.

My brother José offered me work helping him at weekends. For that he gave me something out of his salary and he didn't earn much. But because the plants around there grow in damp and marshy ground, I often had to spend the whole day up to my hips in water. That made me permanently ill. I had to find a family who could pay me something.

After a while I managed to do just that. I thought everything would get better then, because for one thing I was promised a small salary and for another the family only had two children, so I thought there'd probably be less work to do. I dreamed of having more time for school.

But my dreams were shattered very quickly, because the oppression in this family was considerably greater than in the one before. The lady of the house used to complain that I left the saucepans in the kitchen untidy. And I had to scour the saucepans, which were clean anyhow, until they shined, which made my hands bleed. In addition to that, the male members of the family regarded me as "fair game" and often pestered me. It was all too much for me. I left after only four weeks.

Somewhat distraught I started to walk round and round the church in the town one evening praying aloud for God to find a nice family for me. And in just this desperate situation some men came up to me and propositioned me. In such moments, when your very survival is on the line, prostitution is often only a step away. I was aware of the danger. How "easily" I could have earned some money! But I didn't want to do it, because of my religious beliefs. In any case, prostitution would have been the end of the road for me, socially. To get rid of the men, I pretended to be daft in the head. They obviously got frightened, because they cleared off straight away.

That evening I met a woman, an ordinary woman, who'd just lost her husband. She offered me a job looking after her children while she worked in the fields. In the afternoon the children could go to their grandfather. I'd then have the time for school. What could I do? I had no choice, I took the job. But although I only stayed for six months, the time hung heavily on my hands, and I got progressively sicker.

Because the widow was very poor, we couldn't buy enough food for everyone. The children got something to eat at their grandfather's, but that still didn't leave much for me other than water and cassava flour. I also had to sleep with the children, so whenever one of them wet the "bed", I got wet too. I never got any rest. My body's resistance sank lower and lower. Once when I had a bad bout of flu it seemed to me that I was at the end of my tether. There was no one to take care of me. I put a letter to my friend in my suitcase. In the event of my dying she would at least have a last message from me.

Around this time one of my woman teachers put me in touch with a Portuguese couple whose children didn't live at home any more, and I moved in with them. Here I got enough to eat. When I'd recovered some of my strength, I started to go with my friend, the one I'd written the letter to in my desperation, to meetings organised by Catholic nuns. When they found out after a while about my wanting to go to school, they offered me the chance to attend their private school. Gratefully I accepted. They also helped me solve my money problems: I could give religious instruction in state schools. Unfortunately, the Portuguese couple didn't approve, so the nuns found accommodation for me with one of the school's cleaning women. She was a widow and had a child. Her situation as even more hopeless than mine, so I used to give her some of the money I earned and help her with her work.

The school at which I gave religious instruction was a long way from my own school. When I taught there twice a week I didn't even have time for lunch. It was on these days, of all days, that we used to have sport. One day I was so washed-out, yet again, that I collapsed. In the process I injured my foot so badly that I still sometimes get pains there even now. One of the nuns took pity on me and the cleaner. Secretly she sent us the leftovers of meals and the odd bit of clothing. I had hardly any clothes. By then my poor living conditions had weakened me so much that I was suffering from anaemia.

Through my contact with the nuns I began to want to become a nun myself. When I told the mother superior of my wishes she turned me away because of my bad health. She said I should first rest up in my home town, take care of myself and have a break from work. When I was well again I could come back to prepare myself for life in the convent. Although I was bitterly disappointed, I took her advice. But how was I ever going to get back? As usual, I didn't have the necessary funds.

With the help of the nuns, I found my way back to Belém. I was taken in by relations of the Portuguese couple I'd worked for. What now?

It must have been my guardian angel who sent me to this family, because from them I discovered that in certain, special cases the Brazilian air force gives away free flights. With the help of a local padre, I was given permission to take just such a flight to Fortaleza. But as no one could say when I would get a seat, I had to go to the office every day to ask. And so I spent a month like that, tired, ill and almost penniless.

One day when I turned up yet again at the office the woman told me I could fly out in half an hour. I had to spend all my remaining money on a taxi to take me back to the house as quickly as possible for a few of my things and then to rush me to the airport. It was a miracle that I actually arrived in time. I was frightened to death, because I'd never flown before.

I haven't a clue how I got from Fortaleza to my home town. All I know is, I arrived very ill. Luckily, my adoptive parents took me back. But in the village people began telling stories about me. They, and unfortunately my father too, believed that I'd become a prostitute. I couldn't defend myself. I was too exhausted and too ill.

Actually I should have gone to hospital, but I wasn't entitled to INAMPS (the health insurance). The only person who could help me was the padre in our village. He suggested that I should give religious instruction in the town's schools so as to become entitled to health insurance. In this way I was soon able to have the operation that I needed.

I stayed in my home town until the end of 1973. Then I decided to leave again to continue with my education. In any case, I wasn't earning enough. I was a little fitter by now, but my health still wasn't good enough for me to go back to the nuns in Pará.

So, at the beginning of 1974 I decided to go and live with relatives in São Paulo. It was a chance for me to earn more and to go to school, but I also wanted to decide in peace and quiet whether I still wanted to go into the convent. I had just enough money to get to São Paulo. I had to survive the three-day-long journey on just water and the food I'd taken with me.

Life in São Paulo was no picnic. My relatives couldn't keep me, so I had to find work again so that I could go to school. The vicious circle that I'd been through in Pará began again. This time, however, I worked in a chemist's, instead of for a family. Because I'd never learned English, I had terrible problems in school. What's more, the city, the distances from one part to another, the noise and the many dangers exhausted me.

Here too, if I wanted to manage both school and work, I had to get up at 4 a.m. and didn't get home until eleven or twelve at night. After three months I had to give up school. I stayed in the town for another couple of months and then decided to go and stay with my oldest brother, who lived up-country from São Paulo. Unfortunately, I couldn't stay there for long either, because he'd actually decided to go to Maranhao. The easiest thing for me to do was to go with him. Once again I had just enough money for the bus fare.

In Maranhão we lived with my uncle in a small village, and were able to help him in the fields, but once again there was no school for me. Around that time two nuns arrived in the village from Rio Grande do Sul to do missionary work in the North-West. They asked me to help them with their pastoral work and offered me a room in one of their houses. Working with them rekindled my desire to become a nun.

It was then that I began working with herbal medicines. It's almost impossible for poor people to buy pharmaceutical products from chemists' shops, yet Brazil abounds with plants which have healing powers. So, I began to learn about these and to pass my knowledge on to others.

Then I started to have problems again, this time with the nuns. One of them was really jealous that I got on better with the public than she did. It was no wonder, I'd lived the life of the people myself and understood their language and their customs better than a woman from the South. I suffered so much as a result of her jealousy that I got ill again and couldn't work there any longer.

My uncle paid for me to go back to São Paulo. My adoptive mother's mother took me in to look after the house for her. I could barely manage my duties, I was so exhausted and depressed. I no longer had the strength to fight for my life. In fact, I was close to ending it all, because every attempt I made to improve my life seemed to fail.

My relations took me to a psychiatric hospital, where I was treated for a while as an inpatient and later as an outpatient. I had to go to the clinic twice a week — for six months. The doctors explored with me the question of why I wanted to enter the convent. But these conversations weren't much use, since I was usually pumped full of tablets. In the space of six months I was given 1,200 tranquilisers, that's 200 a month. I was so doped-up that all I really did was sleep. I certainly couldn't help around the house.

When one of the nuns from Rio Grande do Sul visited me, I said I wanted to go straight into the convent in order, finally, to find peace. But the mother superior refused, saying that I wasn't suitable in my present state. Once again I'd failed to be accepted by the nuns for health reasons. That made me furious and left me totally without hope. Luckily, though, I'd stayed in touch by letter with the padre in my home town of Ceará. He invited me to go back and work with him in the newly-opened catechesis school. He also advised me not to enter the convent.

So, in the middle of 1977 I returned to Ceará to work as a catechist in the surrounding rural communities. My experience of herbal medicines also proved useful in my work. It was a good job, but the living conditions were poor, and it wasn't long before jealousy arose over who was the padre's favourite.

In 1978 I got permission to go back to live with my adoptive parents. At last I had enough peace and quiet to learn. I prepared myself, through studying at home, for an external exam in Fortaleza, there being no suitable schools in my home. Eventually I was even able to take A Levels. Later I took a theology course with the other catechists.

When my adoptive parents moved to Fortaleza in 1981 I had to look for somewhere of my own to live for the first time in my life. I had to move almost every year because the rents kept rising so dramatically. In the mid-eighties my family helped me buy a cheap house, where I lived with some women friends. My life had apparently become more stable.

But soon after that new quarrels erupted. A few women friends and I had joined the Workers' Party (PT), which had recently set up a branch in our area. We were hoping for some change at last and in the elections for governor supported the PT candidate, who was also a priest. As a result we had problems with our own padre, who didn't think that a man of God should stand for a political post. We suspected, however, that what was behind this were the two men's differing political beliefs, which were plain to see in our work. The nuns continually put obstacles in our way. For example, we didn't get all our letters, and it was only with great dIfficulty that I was able to take part in a pastoral further education course in Salvador.

The conflicts intensified. The church employees also grew more nervous as conflicts became more frequent in the countryside. Our padre had already received death threats. Lots of other problems arose for me at the same time: my father was seriously ill, and I was in debt. With all that, the extra conflict and oppression in the Church was almost unbearable. Despite the padre's attempts at conciliation, I finally asked to be discharged in October 1987.

Since it's almost impossible to find a job outside the Church in our area, I decided to get away once and for all. Mario, one of my many brothers, told me that I might be able to earn a lot of money on the Tucurui Dam in Pará, where he was working. Using the compensation that I'd got from the Church, I set out.

Once again I was bitterly disappointed. Tucurui is a bastion of political and economic power. The area in which the workers live is sealed off and easy to control. No one is allowed to put up visitors — other than wives and children — in the houses. So I lived illegally with Mario. I couldn't find work, because I only had a permit for church work and there were no vacancies. Mario was scared of getting the sack for contravening the ban on visitors. After a month he chucked me out.

What was I supposed to do now? Luckily I still had some money left from my compensation and from the sale of my furniture. I used that to buy a ticket to São Paulo.

Things in my relatives' household had worsened a lot over the years. There were already four families living there by then. But there was nowhere else I could live because the rents were much too high. Finding work was also difficult, because unemployment had risen. I could have found something outside São Paulo, but the minimum wage that I would have earned there would only just have covered my travelling costs. That was pointless. Though I didn't really want to show my weakness by going back home, I decided in this impossible situation to return to the Northeast. I sold the rest of my things to pay for the ticket to Ceará.

First I stayed with relatives in Fortaleza. But it's expensive to live in a city and I wasn't earning. When one day my old friends pressed me to go back to my home village with them I couldn't resist.

Since my house was still occupied I had to stay with friends. I had sold almost all my furniture, so I had to start all over again. After two months I finally found work on an eighteen-month contract at the minimum wage. What will happen after that I can't imagine.'

Recorded by Gerborg Meister

Women and Racism

Black women and racism

The race issue in Brazil is deeply embedded in the country's political, economic, social and cultural structures and must be seen in conjunction with the theory of dependence between the peripheries and the so-called centre countries.

We do not intend to discuss the definition of racism here, nor will we look at the causes of its development during the course of Brazillian history. Instead, we wish to focus on how black women live and cope with it. The well-known term *democracia racial* (democracy of the races, here interpreted as meaning the equality of the skin colours — translator's note), was coined by author Gilberto Freyre (The Masters and the Slaves). It is based on the notion that black and white can co-exist in 'harmony', but essentially reduces the relationship between them to a sexual relationship between black women and white men, without any family formation or obligations. It is an idealisation of the *mae preta* (the 'black mammy'), who is forced to breastfeed the white child while her own child starves. An advertisement used by the Benetton company, which shows a black woman with a white baby at her breast very clearly illustrates this ideology. In protest black women in Brazil have painted over the poster with the slogan 'Wet-nurses — never again'.

What kind of democracy of the skin colours is it when in a Constituent Assembly of 559 not even a dozen of the deputies are black? There are precisely seven[1] deputies belonging to the black race, and of these only four truly represent black interests. Only one of these four is a woman: Benedita da Silva of the Workers' Party (PT). To talk in terms of a *'democracia racial'* in this context is pure demagogy. There is racism in Brazil and it is just as appalling here

1. 1989 figures

as in any other country of the world. Here, however, it has certain special characteristics. A comparison with South Africa, for example, reveals a fundamental difference: in Brazil racism is not embodied in law, yet racism nevertheless affects the lives of black people — men, women and children — in very tangible ways.

There is racism in Brazil. It may have no basis in law, but it is socially organised, whether through employers rejecting woman workers with black skins, authorities refusing to provide public funds to support anti-racist organisations, the publication of school textbooks in which there is massive discrimination against the black race, or through the building of homes with cell-like rooms for domestic servants and of blocks of flats with separate lifts for the (generally black) domestics and staff.

The campaign for the emancipation of slaves and the consequences of its success in 1888 was anything but revolutionary. Apart from a small elite group of black intellectuals, the vast majority of the black population took no part in the process. Their way of rejecting slavery was to escape and set up *quilombos* (villages inhabited by fugitives). In fact, emancipation served the interests of the ruling class, which neither planned nor provided for the incorporation of the former slaves' labour power into the new economic model which it had chosen for Brazil. From the very beginning, since its 'emancipation', the black population has been marginalised. Without going into this more deeply, we should like to pose a question for discussion: can it be a coincidence that around ninety per cent of the inhabitants of most *favelas*, the majority of psychiatric patients, of prison inmates, of the people who lack clothing, food and education are black? The plight of black women should be seen as part of this non-coincidence.

Remember

Just because you
No longer bind me to the stake,
No longer put out my eyes,
No longer hunt me when I flee...

Just because you
No longer feed me from the trough,
And have allowed,
My name to be registered...

Just because you
No longer lash me with the whip,
No longer pierce me with the knife,
No longer stab me in the belly...

That does not mean, you now owe me nothing:
You owe me the key to the slaves' cabin,
Which is hidden in the counter drawer.

Geni Guimarães

Source: *Schwarze Poesie — Poesia Negra. Afrobrasilianische Dichtung der Gegenwart. Portugiesisch-Deutsch*, published by Moema Parente Augel, Edition día, St Gallen/Cologne 1988, p.147

Woman Warrior

Shall I tell you who I am
I come from Minas[1]
I am a daughter of Angola, of Keto and Nago[2]
I'll stand no nonsense.
I sing to the four winds, fear no frailty
For I can fight
Born, raised,
transformed in the Samba
And no one will fell my banner.

João Nogueira

1. Minas Gerais: Brazilian state.
2. Angola, Keto, Nago: African nations.

Historical data

12.4.1500	Europeans arrive in Brazil	
1502-1870	The number of slaves transported to America totals 9,385,315, of which the following percentages were transported to the following countries:	
Brazil	37.7	(3,532,315)
Haiti	9.2	(864,000)
Jamaica	7.9	(748,000)
Cuba	7.5	(702,000)
USA	6.3	(596,000)
13.5.1888	Brazil is the last country to abolish slavery	

Source: *O Negro no Brasil, Da Senzala à Guerra do Paraguai*, by Julio José Chiazenato, São Paulo 1987

The population of Brazil

Year	Whites[1]	Blacks & People of Mixed Blood	Indians	Total
1872	3,787,289	5,756,234[2]	386,955	9,930,478
	38.1%	57.9%	4.0%	100%
1950	32,027,661[3]	19,478,000	329,082	51,834,74
	61.8%	37.6%	0.6%	100%
1990[4]	60,175,000	84,300,000	435,000	145,000,000
	41.5%	58.2%	0.3%	100%

Source: *O Negro no Brasil, Da Senzala à Guerra do Paraguai*, by Julio José Chiazenato, São Paulo 1987

1. including Asians
2. not all were slaves
3. it must be assumed that this includes some blacks who regarded themselves as part of this group
4. author's assessment

Our identity as women and blacks

When we talk about identity we are talking about ourselves as Brazilians living in a society full of contradictions, a society which denies the existence of blacks and aims to make them believe that in order to be human beings they must be white. Obviously, finding an identity in a society such as this is bound to be problematic, and particularly so for a black woman racism, machismo and class distinctions are powerful instruments of control. It is thus part and parcel of this mechanism that people accept their oppression as 'normal' and their 'inferiority' as 'natural'. Notions such as these are passed down through the ideological apparatus, the family, the Church, the media and school. With their help, differences are reinforced and also internalised. The need, the urge to prove the opposite fades visibly. Anyone who fails to conform to the image of the ruler (the white man) is subordinate to him. This is the context in which black Brazilians — who account for at least a third of the 145 million citizens of Brazil — form their identities and develop personalities defined as 'inferior'.

Although fiercely and quite rightly criticised, television is an effective means of keeping the vast majority of the population informed about goings-on in the country and in the world at large. It is the cheapest cinema there is. After a hard day's work the family settles down on the wobbly sofa to watch, with a mixture of delight and expectation, the next episode of a *novela* (soap opera) in which the women and blacks are systematically portrayed as alienated. If the chief protagonist is black, it is not unusual for the role to be played by a blacked-up white actor. On the other hand, the supporting roles — prostitutes, chauffeurs, scoundrels and an army of servants and cleaners — are all played by black actors and actresses.

The *novelas* depict a marvellous world of luxury cars, villas, swimming pools and jetsetting. The entire setting is a refined Hollywood concoction of the kind most often found in cinema cigarette commercials, and the viewers — mostly women — dream of one day emulating their TV heroes and heroines. Advertising too plays its part. Frequently repeated and technically perfect, commercials convey their ideological message with great success. Women are a reliable target audience.

An example. Shampoo adverts in Brazil generally feature women with long, straight, fine, generally blond, hair — the aim being to make the greatest possible impression on black people. But *henne* (a chemical product for straightening hair, not to be confused with henna) is also widely advertised, persuading black women to abuse their natural attributes. Straighten your hair with *henne* and be the perfect (white) woman!

Aesthetic alienation from one's own body affects women in particular. (Frantz Fanon very vividly describes the process whereby blacks attempt to 'make' themselves white, in his book, *Black Skin, White Masks*.) As a rule, black men avoid frizz by wearing their hair very short; in women the alienation is generally more noticeable. When chemical products replaced the hot iron comb, which had hitherto been used to straighten hair, cases of burns to the throat, ears and back increased. Black women now spend more time than ever trying to deny their racial identity: first they have to make up the mixture, then apply it, wait an hour, wash their hair again and so on. Where the process is unsuccessful, they sometimes then resort to still stronger preparations.

Black Brazilian women are not alone in taking such measures. In the Caribbean, and even in Africa itself, for example, in Senegal, a country which contributed much to the theory of negritude (a theory of black awareness), and even in South Africa, where the black population is engaged in a political struggle against apartheid, there are many women who straighten their hair. In the USA too, the country in which the 'black is beautiful' movement was born and where many blacks occupy prominent positions in politics, the economy and the arts, there are still countless black men and women who use chemical products to straighten their hair.

But is this phenomenon explained by the simple fact that there are blacks who envy whites their straight hair, just as there are whites who would rather have frizzy hair? Not at all. To many black women, being white and preferably blond means being better; for white stands for purity, goodness, beauty and intelligence. The black woman, on the other hand, is constantly represented as naive, if not stupid, superstitious, fat and ugly. She always wears an apron and has a scarf on her head. Why should she like being black? Subtly and ingeniously, blacks are being robbed of their identity and find it exceedingly difficult to resist.

As textbooks and television programmes amply demonstrate, even children cannot avoid alienation from their racial identity. The methods employed are always the same: in illustrations, commercials and stories the majority of child protagonists are white and blond. In similar vein, toy shops in Brazil sell only the white version of the Barbie doll — blond with blue eyes — and not the black version which is available in the USA.

Racism is constantly updating its offensive strategies. Let us look, for example, at the way in which language is used: in present-day Brazil the term 'child' refers only to little ones who are blond, wear Johnson & Johnson nappies, drink Nestlé's milk and own Estrela toys. Poor, black children or those from the Northeast are described as 'minors'. 'Society' means the white rich, 'community' means the black poor.

Racism takes countless forms. It is found every day in apparently harmless jokes and games in which every black is called either Pele (after Brazil's best-known black footballer) or Snow White, this being a sarcastic reminder that someone who is black will never match up to the fairy story character of that name. Brazil's cultural racism is equipped with a multitude of nicknames for members of the black race.

Other forms of racism are more serious, such as the arbitrary murder of blacks by paramilitary gangs or 'death squads' such as the 'White Hand' (*Mão Branca*), an organisation associated with the military police. With the aim of eventually 'cleaning up' all criminals, they spread terror in the prisons and murder in the streets. Ninety-eight per cent of their victims are black, often 12 or 13-year-old children. It is also not unusual for workers to be murdered simply for having made themselves unpopular with members of these gangs. Since the authorities have no interest in solving crimes of this kind, dozens of bodies are found in Rio every weekend.

Whites in Brazil are born, grow up and die without ever accepting blacks; blacks are born, grow up and die without ever accepting themselves as blacks. It is as a result of this non-acceptance that the process whereby blacks attempt to 'make' themselves white emerged, was strengthened and, still worse, is constantly renewed.

Of fundamental importance has been the emergence of groups which challenge the status quo on the race issue in Brazil, groups which plan and organise anti-racist campaigns, such as the United Black Movement (MNU). The MNU was founded in São Paulo in 1978, bringing together various anti-racist groups from São Paulo, Rio de Janeiro, Belo Horizonte and other cities. It promotes debate on the issue of racism and is the first movement since the Brazilian Black Front (*Frente Negra Brasileira*), which was active in the 1930s, to have a national profile.

Enough is enough! Black women speak out

Many black women have, at some time or another, had to defend themselves against discrimination. Some have done it loudly, some more quietly. Of those who have remained silent, many have nevertheless offered some kind of resistance in order to help preserve the black race. However, few women have organised politically to fight racial and gender discrimination.

The various black culture groups in general and the MNU in particular deserve ·a certain amount of criticism for their elitism, which runs the risk of destroying the exceptional features of black social and political culture. At the First National Congress of Black Women in March 1989, it was suggested that the planned discussions, seminars and group work be abandoned in favour of something less exclusive, such as workshops on African hair-styles, clothes, music, dance, sport and cookery. These workshops would, it was argued, play a real and practical part in helping black women find and maintain their cultural identity, and to accept themselves as fully valued people with full rights. This 'reflective therapy' would encourage black women to steep themselves body and soul in 'being black', to become aware once again of their history and worth and thus to develop a preparedness to take part in the struggle against racism. For the process whereby blacks attempt to 'make' themselves white, a notion introduced through social, political, religious and economic mechanisms, underpins racism as an instrument of control.

Black and proud

The history of black women in Brazil provides an abundance of themes and heroines of which we can be proud. We should, however, also treat sympathetically those black women who do not wish to preserve their identity as blacks, for letting go of one's identity is always a painful act and a loss. Unlike in the USA, where regardless of the shade of one's skin one is defined as black if one is descended from members of the black race, in Brazil there is, to all intents and purposes, a colour hierarchy. From the lowest rank — black — onwards the sugestion is: the whiter the better. One Brazilian saying suggests 'A white woman for a wedding, a mulata for bed, and a black woman to do the work.' Women whose skin colour is just a little bit lighter will often insist that they are of Indian origin, even when this is untrue and regardless of the fact that in Brazilian society Indians too live only a fringe existence and have, for hundreds of years, been the victims of genocide. At least their skin colour is a little lighter, and they did not, according to historians, allow themselves to be enslaved.

Black women who prefer not to preserve their identity should be told of Aqualtune[1], or Luiza Malin, a fighter who strongly influenced her son, Luiz Gama, the slave-age lawyer who coined the phrase: 'A slave who kills his master is acting in self-defence, whatever the circumstances'. Or asked if they have ever heard of the many other still-unknown women slaves, of those, for example, who repeatedly had abortions in order that they should never bear slave children. They should be reminded of the former women slaves who sought refuge in *quilombos* (villages occupied by fugitive slaves) throughout Brazil and who fought to the death to defend them.

1. During a slave hunt the kingdom of Canjanga in the Congo was invaded. An army of ten thousand, led by the king's daughter Aqualtune, fought back. Defeated and captured, Aqualtune was transported to Recife as a slave. Pregnant from having been raped, she was sold to a sugar-cane plantation near Porto Calvo (now in the state of Alagoas). There she got word of the Quilombos dos Palmares, and heavily pregnant, led the escape to Palmares of several slaves. Alongside the Ganga Zumba (the Great Lord), she organised the fugitives' village and began to work towards the founding of a black state. (Palmares existed for 67 years and had up to 20,000 inhabitants.) Later one of her daughters gave her a grandson: Zumbi dos Palmares, a hero and role model for black Brazilians (he is remembered on 20 November).

Naturally the system does not contribute to keeping our history alive. Much has been lost and forgotten. We should however, mention Maria de Lourdes V. Nascimento, who in May 1950 founded the National Council of Black Women, and Elsa de Souza, who at around the same time, set up the Domestic Servants' Association. We might also mention several women who during the seventies and eighties were active in political organisations such as the Workers' Party (PT) and the MNU: deputy Benedita da Silva (PT — Rio), Professor Lélia Gonzalez and journalist Pedrina de Deus (both from Rio), and sociologist and national coordinator of MNU, Luiza Barrios (Bahia). Many other equally important women are helping to raise consciousness throughout the land. These days, in almost every Brazilian state, there are a variety of organisations and initiatives championing the rights of black women, in which women are involved, swap experiences, learn together how to grow and how to develop strategies to help them survive better in their daily struggle.

Feminism and black women

The Brazilian women's movement has gone a long way towards building a non-Marxist version of history. It has moved the debate on sexuality forward and in this way, at least, is attempting to address women as a whole. To this extent it deserves our praise and solidarity. However, it is this very lack of specificity which makes it difficult for us to identify the political and ideological struggle in which Brazilian women — black and white — are engaged as just that, struggle.

It is, of course, vitally important that black women become involved in the struggle against the three-fold discrimination to which they are exposed — as blacks, as women and as poor people. These three factors of oppression are closely linked, and the only solution is an overall solution. In Brazil one cannot, for example, talk in terms of one female identity for both black and white women. Until the women's movement accepts the signficance of both of these groups, it will continue to make the mistake of allowing the complex nature of Brazil's social relations to go unconsidered. For example, Brazilian women won the right to vote in 1934, but not until 1989 was the right extended to illiterates. That means that the majority of black women were not allowed to exercise their rights for fifty years. Different experiences cannot be generalised. Even making the link back to our slavery, a slavery which continued after emancipation and strictly speaking still exists today, is unreliable. The reason that black women — even if they do not consciously perceive the discrimination against them as being three-fold — regard the question of race as more important than the question of gender is that their oppression within Brazilian society is not derived from biological sexual distinctions — a black woman's vagina does not differ anatomically from that of a white woman — but clearly from racial and social distinctions.

The fact that the black man was enslaved along with the black woman prevented him from developing an oppressive but at the same time protective attitude towards her, as happened in relationships between white partners (although he did later follow his white brother's lead in this respect). On the other hand, in mixed relationships black women were oppressed by white men, but not protected.

It is important to realise that the white woman's struggle largely concentrates on gaining equality with the white man. After all, her position in society has always been a superior one, not only in comparison with black women, but with black men. Throughout history black women have always been the losers. It is for this reason that they have tended to develop strategies for resistance and survival which are unfamiliar to white women.

The major criticism levied at the women's movement by black women's groups is that it fails to give sufficient priority to the question of race. The women's movement ignores the fact that around 50 per cent of Brazilian women are black, the majority of them living in poverty, and has so far neglected the inequality of opportunity which exists between black and white women in all spheres of social, economic and political life. In short, it does nothing to challenge the white race's preservation of its racial privileges. Consequently, one particular exchange from 1984 between a black and a white would still be possible at a women's meeting today: 'In my opinion there are no differences between us: if my servant girl doesn't turn up for work, I go to the sink and wash up myself.' 'Our situations aren't even vaguely comparable: apart from the fact that I'm my own servant girl. I don''t have either a sink or water in my home.'

White woman/black woman — in Brazil these terms are defined not by skin colour, but by the huge differences which exist in the quality of life they enjoy.

Black and black woman

The whip cracked — I screamed, wept, struggled,
But they called my resistance cowardice
Indolence
They attacked me and locked me up
I'm black, still black, but only in colour
I've tried my best to become white
As white as you like
Black and white, right?
Today the whip is my wage
The belt which I must fasten tighter
I scream, weep, struggle
But they call my resistance insurrection
Outrage
They turned me against myself, made me white
But I'm black, still black, and not just in colour
I know I'll get out, out of madhouses and hospitals
Of prisons and youth detention centres
I'll escape from the kitchen and the streets
I'll win, I'll be black
As black as you don't like
Black and black, *Zé!*

Bibliography

Carneiro, Sueli and Theresa Santos, *Mulher Negra*, Nobel Conselho Estadual da Condição Feminina, 1985

Chiavenato, Julio José, *O Negro no Brasil, Da Senzala à Guerra do Paraguai*, Livaria Brasiliense Editora SA, 1987

Maioria Falante, Ano IV — No 19, Junho/Julho 1990

Ministério da Educação-Fundação de Assistência ao Estudante Instituto de Recursos Humanos João Pinheiro-BH, Educação e Discriminação dos Negros, 1988

Movimento Negro Unificado 1978 — 1988, 10 anos de Luta Contra o Racismo, Salvador/Bahia

Nascimento, Abdias do, *O Negro Revoltado*, Editora Nova Fronteira, 1982

Nzinga Informativo, Ecos do I Encontro Nacional de Mulheres Negras, março de 1988

Relatório I Encontro de Mulheres Negras de Belo Horizonte 1981

Relatório II Encontro de Mulheres Negras do Estado da Bahia, 21 a 23 out/1988

São Paulo em Perspectiva — *Negro*, SEADE abril/junho 1988

Anna Lúcia Florisbela dos Santos

I am cheaper

Muchacha...

I am the washing machine
which the Señor won't buy
as long as I wash cheaper and save the señora
time
and her hands
rough skin;

I am the vacuum cleaner
which the Señora doesn't need,
the car wash,
the nursery school,
the laundry,
the sick ward,
the shopping trolley;

I am the Señora's
emancipation,
the button
which fulfills every wish — just press me;

I am cheaper...

Source: *Muchacha — Die unsichtbaren Dienerinnen Lateinamerikas*, edited by
Reinhardt Jung, Lamuv Taschenbuch 28.

Black women in the city

Black women, strong women, women warriors, where do you get your strength?

'All women are raised first and foremost to marry, to have a husband and children. Yet history has demonstrated that the black woman only has the right to children, that no marriage takes place and that she is ultimately the head of the family.' (Batista)

Black women are forced either to provide for their children alone or to help their partners do so. The first stage in a black woman's survival strategy is to find a *favela* in which to make her home, in a hut cobbled together from planks of wood, cardboard and tin and under the most difficult of conditions (without drinking water, without drainage). The living conditions endured by black women in Brazil are the cause of considerable deficiences in the areas of education and training, and are therefore crucial factors in reducing their chances of finding a decent job.

Consequently, many black women try to produce goods or services themselves, primarily in the informal sector. Younger women tend to concentrate on the beauty sector, working as manicurists, pedicurists or hairdressers. Once they have mastered basic arithmetic, they seek work as cashiers in supermarkets or as bus conductresses. Many earn a living as dressmakers, washerwomen or ironing women, since these kinds of work enable them to work at home or at the customer's home.

Street trading is also an activity frequently carried out by black women. There are not many goods which can be produced for sale by the seller herself without a great deal of expenditure. Any woman found selling such goods (generally food, since it is rare for losses to be made on food — what is not sold is consumed at home) runs the risk of being picked up by health officials or trade supervisors.They either find fault with the hygienic conditions under which her goods are produced or demand a trading licence, the procurement of which is a lengthy and expensive business — after all, there's Brazilian bureaucracy to contend with!

In towns like Rio de Janeiro, São Paulo and Belo Horizonte, where hundreds of woman street traders offer their goods for sale, the actual business is often carried out by proper firms. These firms are huge 'alternative' companies with well-organised transport and distribution networks. They buy their products wholesale at low prices and deliver them to the street traders for resale. They also employ checkers to supervise the selling. In the late afternoon the takings are counted, the sellers paid and the unsold goods reloaded. It is, in fact, just another way of exploiting unqualified workers, of competing with established shops and their employees, of circumventing tax and duty legislation and thus of reducing costs — once again at the expense of society's poorest and most needy.

The majority of the jobs open to black women are still for paid housework[1], for example, as cooks, kitchen-maids, cleaning women, charwomen, nannies and 'general helps'. Although in theory black women could also do some of these jobs in hotels and restaurants, such establishments prefer white women. Consequently, the labour market is limited instead to the households of well-off (mainly white) families.

Under Brazilian law employers are required to pay unskilled workers a minimum wage. The major criticism here is that this minimum wage is far less than a living wage and does not even guarantee a worker's family basic foodstuffs. If housework were an occupation like any other, then domestic servants would do their work and be paid more or less reasonably, like other workers. Yet the life of a domestic servant is pure hell.

Slavery was abolished in Brazil in 1888. We are approaching the end of the twentieth century, yet black domestic servants are still there to serve their masters, their children, relations and guests, to fulfill their most banal wishes and to do all kinds of hard labour. Many families do without a washing machine simply because they have a servant to see to the washing for them. Nor is it uncommon for servants to have to give in to sexual harassment by the men in the house.

On Brazil's informal hierarchical ladder the domestic servant occupies the bottom rung. She is the natural successor to the woman slave, someone whom everyone can treat as badly as they like. If she is dissatisfied, the most she can do is look for a new job, although even then she knows in advance that it will not be appreciably different from the last. A domestic servant has no rights, just duties.

As they become increasingly aware of being exploited, domestic servants are becoming increasingly dissatisfied with this situation. More and more are becoming organised.

In 1988 the Constitutional Assembly voted to extend the scope of Brazilian labour law to paid housework. The Chamber of

1. Paid housework as opposed to the unpaid housework which almost all women do as part of the process of reproducing labour power.

Deputies debated the question of regulating paid housework as if the subject were totally new. In fact, the same debate had already been conducted once before, almost 50 years ago, and with very few differences; back in 1941 campaigns demanding an end to the social injustice faced by domestic servants prompted the government to introduce statutory regulation number 3851, which guaranteed domestics eight days notice of dismissal, 20 days annual leave and one day off each week (Sunday or another day, as agreed). Yet some servants still work on Sundays and are not permitted to go out until lunch is over. The statutory regulation was never incorporated into Brazilian labour law. It has even been sabotaged by the courts responsible for labour law through their vigorous support of the employers.

Ten years later in 1950, the founding of the Domestic Servants' Association and the holding of the First Congress of Braziiian Blacks reopened the debate. The black woman lawyer Guiomar de Mattos conducted a review of the statutory regulation and made a number of suggestions for its improvement: by restricting the number of hours worked by domestic servants each day to a maximum of ten with a one and a half hour break; in the case of dismissal, by giving domestics who have worked in a household for more than ten years the right to compensation; by granting domestics pension rights and access to health insurance and other social welfare benefits. Congress condemned cases in which the law had not been adhered to and opposed the requirement that domestic servants register with the police before they can be granted a work permit. '... you see, the police are responsible for domestic servants... They say that work is a right, but for domestic servants it's clearly an offence, since they first have to go to the police to register.' (Rodrigues Alves)

In 1972 the subject was once again placed on the legislative agenda, with the result that domestic servants' employment conditions were regulated that year in a law (Number 5859) and in 1973 in a statutory regulation (Number 71885). Yet still the legal provisions exist only on paper.

In 1981 the Fourth Domestic Servants' Congress was held, with 208 delegates from 13 Brazilian states taking part.

Their principal demand was once again — that regulations governing paid housework be incorporated into Brazilian labour law. They also demanded that the 13 associations represented be recognised as legitimate representatives for the purposes of setting up a trade union for paid houseworkers.

In 1988 domestic servants finally won the right to a day off each week, to a thirteenth monthly wage packet each year, health insurance, pensions and more besides — welfare benefits to which every other worker in Brazil was already entitled. Loud protests were made, highlighting the existence of racism in Brazil and once again confirming that the black woman and white woman'a struggles are not the same.

Domestic servants are now in danger once again of being tricked out of the fruits of their struggle and not employed in accordance with the law. For even though Brazil's deputies have been convinced, albeit 50 or 100 years late, of the necessity for these measures, that is not at all the case with the employers. They refuse to treat domestic servants as human beings with equal rights by paying them higher wages. They argue instead, that 'a girl like this who works in a factory has, after all, considerable expenses. She has to pay travelling expenses and rent, to buy clothes and much more besides. All her wages go on things like that... If, on the other hand, she works here in the house for us, she eats what we eat... And she wears a uniform, which we provide. And if we can give her the odd thing, then we do that too, a pair of almost new shoes, for example...'

'I prefer a type which no longer exists these days: the humble domestic servant... like we had in my parents' home, in a small town... These days they're insolent, rebellious and want to do all the things that we do...'

'I prefer to employ someone who's somewhat darker than I am, so that the difference is immediately clear. I don't think a servant should have the same colour skin as her mistress... because that can cause confusion. People come and can't tell at first glance which is the housewife and which is the maid...' (Ary Farias)

Another argument used by many of the employers who pay less than the minimum wage is based on the untenable claim that they employ women from the country's poorest regions in the Northeast, women who have never been to school and who would have starved had they not been lucky enough to meet them (the employers) (*Veja*, 4.1.1989) This is just one of the many ways in which employers attempt to justify the way they treat their domestics. They believe that second-hand shoes are the best present that anyone could give, compliance the best quality that anyone could have, and they raise racial discrimination to the level of a criterion on which to base their choice of domestics. It is a tough punishment indeed for women who have had no other opportunities in life.

There is no effective way of checking whether domestic servants are being employed in accordance with the law, nor will there ever be. It is left to them to accept or reject their employers' continuing violation of the law. It will be many years before all of them are informed about their rights. It is noticeable, however, that a growing number of women prefer to work in factories and for cleaning companies where they can earn more and get welfare benefits and where they do not have to put up with the pathological authoritarianism of 'madam'.

For blacks in general and black women in particular the fact that paid housework is now regulated by law is a victory. But the battle is not yet won. The fight goes on. First and foremost in order to ensure that the laws which have been passed are also adhered to. After that there are many improvements which will have to be fought over, for example, the creation of job-training projects for black workers, for the race issue to be debated within the trade unions and for government anti-racism policies to be implemented at local, state and national level. There is a lot to do. Let's make a start!

Bibliography

Deus, Pedrina de, *O Trabalho Doméstico é o mais importante do país*, mimeographed, no year

Farias, Zaira Ary, *Domesticidade 'Cativeiro Feminino?'*, Achiamé/CMB, 1983

Maioria Falante (Jurema Batista), May/June 1980

Nascimento, Abdias do, *O Negro Revoltado*, Editora Nova Fronteira, 1982

Veja, Editora Abril from 27 April 1988, 11 May 1988 and 4 January 1989

Anna Lúcia Florisbela dos Santos

Women and Religion

The Day Labourer

Boarded on a lorry
she sets off very early;
without security
she'll try
to earn her daily bread.

The boss bought a tractor,
a lorry and harrow
he sent her away her —
now she's unemployed
no longer needed
in the fields.
All she wanted was a full stomach,
now she's a *bóia-fria*.

She tried to improve her family's lot,
and moved one day
full of optimism to the town.
But the hunger for pleasure remained,
and so she tries,
to earn the family's keep.

Neither farm-
nor factory-worker,
she earns a wretched wage,
but still she laughs.
She never has anything left out of her little bit of money, she does all kinds
of work
and laughs in order not to cry.

Already she has earned her land glory and honour,
but she is no longer allowed to work
the land, which she loves so much.
Now I ask, of any who hear:
For whom did God create the world
Was it for the few
or for us?

Maria, Maria
'O, Dona Maria, como vai?'
— 'Hey, Maria, how's it going?'

So many women in Brazil are called Maria after the Virgin Mary that this greeting almost always fits. Maria is ever-present, on the street, in the houses, in songs, among women. She is on everybody's lips and hailed in every breath: *'Nossa Senhora!'* (Our Lady), *'Vixe!'* (*Virgem* — Virgin).

The European image of Mary was exported to Brazil along with the Roman Catholic Church: the holy, entranced, blue-eyed, obedient, asexual Mary. For centuries the Church used this image of ideal womanhood to foster the subordinate role of women. This Mary still determines the devoutness of the people, morality and the image of the perfect woman.

Catholicism and the African cultures brought by the slaves came together in South America. In the Afro-Brazilian religions there are many gods and goddesses (*Orixás*) who, with their human traits and attributes, closely resemble real people. The fusion of the official Roman Catholic devotion to Mary with African religions produced a multi-faceted Brazilian Mary.

Mary is the Brazilians' secret goddess, the *'mae do povo'* (mother of the people). It is sometimes impossible to distinguish the adoration of Mary from that of the sea goddess *Iémanja* or the mother goddess *Oxúm*.

Brazil's Catholic patron saint is *Maria Aparecida* (Our Lady of the Vision). She is personified by a black statue which fishermen found in their nets in the eighteenth century. *Aparecida* quickly became the protectress of slaves.

Mary is ever present in the daily lives of the women of the *povo*. Brazilian women can identify with her — she is one of them: she is poor, her husband is a simple craftsman; she has no home in which to bear her child, but gives birth in a hut, she is a migrant from the interior and has to go to Bethlehem, from there to flee to Egypt. Mary is a woman of the *povo*; black, starving, struggling. Mary is pregnant 'out of wedlock', exposed to the scorn of society. Mary is a mother. Nor does Mary's virginity any longer merely symbolise her asexuality and therefore her distance from the reality of other women's lives. For women who all too often experience sexuality as violence, as rape, Mary's virginity symbolises the dream of physical autonomy.

Mary, the Accessible, the woman of the people, mediates between an unapproachable god and women. She is present always and everywhere. It is to her that accusations, calls for support and help, vows and hymns are directed.

Mary, we have no beans,
nothing to eat today.
Mary, we have no bread,
but bills aplenty.
Mary, we have no medicine,
no one can live like this.
Mary, Mother of God, resolute lady,
example of faith and deliverance,
help us, Mother Mary, to turn water into wine
and into bread, to fill our poor bellies.
Show us, Mary, how to establish the Kindom of God.

Mary, we want to go away,
where, we do not know.
Mary, each day
we struggle for deliverance.

Help us, Mother Mary, to defeat oppression.
Teach us, Mary, that life is lived
through struggle and not through fear.

As base Christian communities spread and raise awareness among the poor, this image of Mary is gaining in importance: a woman from the povo, always present in the daily lives of Brazilian women. Mary is becoming a companion and liberator in the people's struggle, the *companheira na luta do povo*. The women involved in the struggle sing the hymn which Mary sang, in which she proclaimed the approach of a just society saying, 'And my spirit hath rejoiced in God my Saviour. For he hath regarded the low estate of his handmaiden: for, behold, from henceforth all generations shall call me blessed... He hath put down the mighty from their seats, and exalted them of low degree. He hath filled the hungry with good things; and the rich he hath sent empty away.' (Luke, Chapter 1)

Mary participated actively in the struggle for a just society and is hence becoming a role model for and comrade-in-arms of the women who organise at grassroots level.

Christiane Fröhlich and Erika Füchtbauer

Negra Mariama — **Black Mary**

Negra Mariama summons us to trim the banner ready for showing:
the image of *Aparecida* in our slavery
with the face of the common people,
the colour of our skin.

Negra Mariama summons us to sing
God has united the weak, that they might free themselves.
And cast the great landowners from their thrones
who had enslaved for fun.

Negra Mariama summons us to dance,
sarava! Hope until the sunrise.
In the samba we see the spilled blood,
hear the screams and silence of the martyrs.

Negra Mariama summons us to fight
in our movement, without losing heart.
She lifts the heads of the dispossessed,
our *Companheira* summons us to carry on.

Christiane Fröhlich and Erika Füchtbauer

Women in base Christian communities

The Church is the people organising themselves,
is the oppressed in search of liberation
in Jesus Christ, of resurrection.

In the sixties the Catholic Church experienced change from below through the emergence of base Christian communities.

A base Christian community is one in which laymen and women assume responsibility for and take over the organisation of the life of the community. They tend to develop in the poorer quarters of towns or in rural areas where just a few priests are responsible for several communities which are therefore sometimes left to their own devices for long periods. In such areas the people often begin to meet together without the guidance of priests, to worship, for Bible readings and for discussion purposes.

The 'base' is the poor and oppressed in Brazilian society. People come together in base Christian communities with a need to unite their spiritual and practical daily concerns. In Brazil, the common struggle for survival is always also a political struggle.

The people, who struggle,
tired of the lies,
tired of the suffering,
tired of the waiting.
The people, who struggle,
tired of the waiting,
seeking deliverance.

Something rarely remarked upon in accounts of base Christian communities is that they are for the most part sustained by women. First there are the countless nuns who live and work with people at grassroots level in *favelas* and on housing estates on the outskirts of towns. Many base Christian communities can be traced back to nuns' initiatives — in Brazil there are considerably more nuns than priests or monks. ·

Then there are the women from the *povo*, who coordinate Bible study groups, organise and lead religious services and give the children religious instruction. Women also meet in the mothers' clubs, the *clube de maes*, which form the nucleus of many base Christian communities.

Reading together and interpreting Bible texts, even without the help of a priest, is an important part of meetings in the base Christian communities. The Bible is an essential tool in the consciousness-raising process.

The methods employed in Bible study may be summed up in three words: seeing — judging — acting. The first step is to examine the reality of group members' lives and to talk over problems. In this way they are able to relate their own lives to the Bible. During the second stage the group reads a text from the Bible and tries to learn from it about various aspects of their own lives, including the structures created by oppression and poverty. Finally comes the search for ways to improve their lives. These might include demonstrating in front of the town hall in order to get mains water and electricity for a *favela*, occupying land or simply talking to someone.

Another essential part of this joint venture is the religious service, which allows the people to draw fresh hope for their struggle from their faith.

The people in base Christian communities frequently come up against the limits imposed by the Church's patriarchal structure: men occupy the leading positions, and if the local bishop is conservative in his approach then life can prove difficult for the community. Another limit is the Church's sexist moral standards. Even basic issues such as sexuality, contraception, abortion and sexual violence are taboo for the majority of women.

Despite these limits, the active participation of women in base Christian communities represents a step towards emancipation. How is this possible in a Church which has traditionally oppressed and still oppresses women? 'My husband lets me go to church. If I want to go somewhere else, for example, to a union meeting, then that's much more difficult.' Community meetings are the only opportunity that many women get to escape home and hearth. Here they meet other women with whom they can talk; they experience solidarity and learn to recognise their plight. For illiterate women, learning to read and write is an important step in the process of political emancipation. When they start to organise together in their own districts, they begin to feel this much more concretely. The base Christian community is a place where women become conscious that they are part of the story.

Christiane Fröhlich and Erika Füchtbauer

Women and the Law

Women and violence

The following story was told by eighteen-year-old Renata: 'Once upon a time there was a girl called Mariazinha and a boy called Joãozinho. They were going out together, but Mariazinha's mother wasn't having it and forbade it. Then they had to get married because he'd taken advantage of her.

After a while Joãozinho began to beat Mariazinha. He used to hit her around the head, on the nose, in the stomach, in the eyes, all over. And he destroyed all her clothes. Then he left her.

She started seeing another man. He hit her as well and then left her, and then there was another one, and he hit her and left her too. And so it went on: hold tight — leave — hold tight — leave. Well, do you like my story?'

An everyday account of the lives of Brazilian women?

For those who want more proof of the violence to which women are exposed every day, one glance at the headlines in a newspaper should suffice: '*Pistoleiro* killed wife with gun!', 'Woman shot out of jealousy.'

Take Nova Iguaçu. Some of Brazil's cities, responding to pressure from women's organisations, have set up police stations exclusively for women; Nova Iguaçu is not one of them. In this town of two million inhabitants near Rio women are still fighting for such institutions.

On the 8th of March 1987 the local women's movement collected 1,200 signatures calling for a women's police station. Such a station is particularly necessary for the women of Nova Iguaçu because the town has the highest crime rate in Brazil. Yet not until July 1989 did the mayor finally agree even to meet the women. To add weight to their demand, thirteen different women's groups, from mothers' groups to the Domestic Servants' Association to women students' groups, handed the mayor 5,000 signatures, along with an analysis of the official statistics on crimes against women.

Even though officially recorded crimes reflect only a fraction of the actual violence to which women are exposed each day, the analysis revealed the following figures: in the months of April and May 1989, 339 cases of violence against women were recorded in Nova Iguaçu, four each day. In general, 70 per cent of all cases relate to bodily harm, 5 per cent are rapes and 4 per cent killings. The victims (in 70 per cent of all recorded cases) were women aged between 15 and 40. The majority of acts of violence (52 per cent) were carried out in the home. Attacks on the streets accounted for only 28 per cent of recorded cases. Eighty-three per cent of the attackers knew their victims personally. They were husbands, lovers and friends.

The statistics which the police compile on these crimes are totally inadequate, a sign perhaps that explaining the motives and discovering the nature of the offenders is of no importance in official circles. Violence against women is still a minor offence, jealousy a socially accepted motive. In the view of the women's movement in Nova Iguaçu, the situation is particularly difficult when the attacker is a member of the victim's own family (54 per cent of cases). In such cases the woman is often emotionally and economically dependant on the attacker, and that prevents her from reporting offences. Yet even if she separates from her husband, she is still not safe from his attacks. It is not uncommon for a man to continue to pursue, threaten and commit acts of violence against his wife for many years, regardless of whether she is living independently or in another relationship.

The percentage of crimes which go undetected is very high, and not merely because women fear reporting members of their own families; women also have difficulty in explaining their plight to male police officers, since the police do not see them as victims, but regard mistreated women instead as 'easy women', there for the having. Consequently, the mistreatment is often resumed by the police.

For these reasons, women's groups in the cities have fought for the establishment of women's police stations. The stations are staffed entirely by women and work with a variety of social services to help battered women. Here, victims can talk openly about what has happened to them. In cases of bodily harm and rape, the often completely terrified women are also given help by the medical services. In addition, the women who staff the stations collect statements from witnesses in order to prepare a case and see it through court. The objective is to have the attacker punished, for all too often in the past men accused of such crimes have been acquitted, despite having clearly committed a crime.

The law says, for example, that someone who kills can receive a prison sentence of between six and twenty years. However, it has been quite usual for the Brazilian legal system to justify the murder of a woman in terms of it having been necessary to save the man's honour. Offenders have thus frequently been acquitted.

Accordingly, another of the objectives pursued by the women's police stations and the women's movement is to run educational campaigns explaining that the use of violence against women is a criminal act. People must also, they say, be made to realise that verbal abuse and coercion are punishable offences.

It is not enough, of course, for these women to encourage female victims to report men for crimes committed. The various women's groups in Nova Iguaçu are also demanding the establishment of women's refuges. Battered women could then be given information about refuges to which they could go if they can no longer go on living with their attackers. The refuges would offer protection from further attacks.

Although they are a step in the right direction for city women, in the light of the rising number of acts of violence in recent years it is clear that women's police stations can only check some of the problems.

For women living in the countryside, where there are as yet no women's police stations, the situation is even more alarming. In addition to violence within the family, violence motivated by the growing number of conflicts over land is also on the increase. Crops are destroyed, houses burned down and women and children threatened in order to force them to divulge the whereabouts of their men. The methods employed by the large landowners in rural areas to demonstrate their power have even included sexual abuse and attacks on pregnant women.

'Two cars without number plates drew up, a blue Fiat and a light-coloured Passat. In the blue Fiat sat a police officer by the name of Lima, who asked after my husband. I said he was working at the moment. My five children were around me, and I began to get scared. We were in my neighbour's house. A bit later Lima came back and tried to make me get into his car, but I refused, so he grabbed my seven-year-old in order to wring out of me where Antonio, my husband, was.'

'I, Teodolina, a widow and mother of four, have become a victim because of something which belongs to me. I was left these 130 hectares of land by my husband. The *fazendeiro* (landowner) banned me from working on half of my land. He said it was his land, and that I couldn't sell it. I've already been attacked by this *fazendeiro* and the policeman in the *fazendeiro's* office.'

In order to encourage women throughout Brazil to report acts of violence committed against them, women's groups have declared the 10th of October a day of action against violence against women.

Gerborg Meister

Constitution and reality
Women and labour law

Brazilian women are discriminated against on the labour market at all levels. There are laws, but only on paper. In recent years, however, woman workers have mobilised on a large scale to struggle for their rights.

The rights of woman workers on the land and in the towns are set out in Article 7 of chapter two of the Brazilian Federal Constitution. Yet in the day-to-day operation of the 'dog-eat-dog' capitalist system these rights are not respected. Article 7, Paragraph 30, for example, states that 'It is forbidden to discriminate in respect of remuneration, the type of work carried out and terms of employment on the grounds of sex, age, skin colour, marital status and so on.'

Reality is rather different; discrimination is the first thing that women learn about at the start of their working lives. Early in the process of finding new staff companies apply a variety of criteria to ensure that they select the right kind of women workers: age (not over 30), skin colour (preferably white) and marital status (single and without children). Future female employees are also required to undergo pregnancy tests and many companies demand sterilisation certificates. In this way employers avoid having to finance a whole range of legally guaranteed welfare benefits.

A woman over the age of 30 is likely to have great difficulty finding a job in the service sector, since she no longer conforms to the ideological and mythical model of the young, beautiful, attractive woman. If, in addition, she is black, then she has absolutely no chance of getting the job, since her skin colour is completely at variance with the predominant racist ideology.

Those women who manage to overcome these hurdles and find a job then find new obstacles placed in their paths, for every company develops an internal mechanism to mask unequal pay for men and women doing the same work. There is no lack of arguments advanced in the employers' defence, for example, that it is traditionally the man's job and duty to feed his family.

The inevitable consequence is that the company considers the man's work more important and values it more highly. At AEG-Telefunken, for example, a male packer who is a sole-breadwinner gets a bonus on top of his basic wage. A female colleague in the same department does not get that bonus, even if she has to provide for her family alone. She is not recognised as the head of the family.

Physically demanding work is rated more highly and better paid, while the skills which are seen as typically feminine skills, such as dexterity and speed, are placed in the lowest wage bands.

In 1987 women earned on average less than 50 per cent of the male average wage and represented 34.7 per cent, more than a third, of the working population. These figures are taken from a study carried out by the Brazilian Institute of Geography and Statistics (IBGE), which established that equal pay only exists in the lower wage bands; higher salaries — 20 times the minimum wage or more — are almost exclusively a male privilege.

Another entrepreneurial method for devaluing the work of women and women's wages consists of taking women on as unskilled labour, but then deploying them in sectors requiring a qualification: for example, a qualified radio technician applied for a vacant post with AEG-Telefunken. The company took the woman on as unskilled labour for a correspondingly lower wage, but then used her in the vacant technician's post. In this way woman workers are forced to sell their labour power at less than the market price.

One of the major gains that women have made is the right to maternity leave of 120 days without loss of pay or position (Article 7, Paragraph 28 of the Federal Constitution). Yet in practice this right has lost many women their jobs. Even before it was passed firms were demanding that would-be employees undergo pregnancy tests. Those that were taken on then had to undergo humiliating checks each month. Any who became pregnant were dismissed immediately.

Recently the situation has become even more difficult. Before the introduction of maternity leave the number of Brazilian women who had been sterilised was alarmingly high, but it is now noticeable that firms are demanding sterilisation certificates more frequently (see, Having children? That's our decision!, p.81).

The presence of women in the workplace, their participation in the work of various movements and the opening of a debate on feminism and women's rights are linked, both in terms of timing and content, with the struggle which is underway in Brazilian society for full civil rights.

Maria Cecília Camargo

Improvements in the legal status of women in the new Brazilian Constitution

Section I — Rights and fundamental guarantees
— Equality before the law without reservation; men and women shall have equal rights and duties within the meaning of this constitution (Art. 50).

Section II — Social rights
— Rights for urban and rural workers, whose principal objectives are to see improvements in their social conditions (Art 70):
— Paid maternity leave of 120 days without loss of job or pay
— Paternity leave in accordance with legal provision.
— Protection of the women's labour market through legal measures to be determined individually.
— Free care for children and dependents from birth up to the age of six in crèches and pre-school groups.
— A ban on unequal pay, demarcation and employment conditions on grounds of sex, age or marital status.
— Domestic servants shall be guaranteed the following already existing rights and entitlements: the right to receive the legal minimum wage, inalterability of wages other than in line with settlements or industrial agreements, wages paid on the basis of a thirteen-month-year, one day off each week with pay, the right to paid annual leave, maternity leave of 120 days and a pension.
— The right to social insurance benefits for housewives.

Section VIII — Economic (and financial) order
— With reference to urban areas: title to property and rights of use may be conferred on the man, woman or both, regardless of marital status (Art. 183 Para. 10).
— With reference to agriculture, land ownership, agrarian reform: title to property and rights of use may be conferred on the man, the woman or both, regardless of marital status, as set out and stipulated in law (Art. 189).

Section VII — Social order
— The family, as the basis of society, shall enjoy the special protection of the state. Also under state protection shall be any stable common law marriage between a man and a woman who

are recognised as a family. The law shall facilitate the conversion of such a relationship into a marriage (Art. 226 Para. 0).

— The rights and duties attached to marriage shall be observed by husband and wife alike.

— Legal equality with legitimate children for illegitimate and adopted children.

Women and the Fight for Rights

'Having children? That's our decision!' The women's health movement and population policy

Since the early 1980s a great number of women's health centres and groups have been established all over Brazil, groups such as the *SOS Corpo da Mulher* in Recife and the *Colectivo de Sexualidade e Saúde* in São Paulo. The women's health movement aims firstly to make it possible for women to discuss and learn about their bodies, their health and their sexuality, and secondly to fight, through public campaigns, for health care provision and the right of women to make their own decisions about their bodies.

In view of the health problems caused by hormonal methods of contraception, back-street abortions and attempts to make sterilisation the main form of contraception for women, reproductive rights are a crucial issue. It is not merely a matter of the individual woman's right to choose how many children she has. More importantly, it is a question of creating the social conditions which will actually make a free choice possible — not only nursery provision, legal protection for expectant and nursing mothers and an end to sexual oppression, but also access to and information about safe forms of contraception and safe abortions. As it attempts to address these issues, the women's health movement is having to counter not only the Catholic Church's and both left- and right-wing nationalists' condemnation of contraceptive provision and abortion, but also the authoritarian practices of private population control organisations.

From the beginning there were those within the military governments in power after 1964 who were willing to go along with the attempts, at the time primarily of the US, to implement a population control policy in Brazil. However, such a policy could not possibly be official government doctrine, since the whole idea of population control was grossly inconsistent with the military's nationalist vision of Brazil as a major power and also with its plans to colonise the Amazon region. A straightforward birth control policy was also incompatible with the views of an important social force within the country, the Catholic Church. Although the military's official line was that population growth was good for economic growth and facilitated the geostrategic protection of 'empty spaces', it nevertheless permitted a large number of foreign-funded private organisations with population control programmes to establish themselves in Brazil.

The oldest and by far the largest of these organisations is the Civil Society for Family Welfare (BEMFAM), founded in 1965, which is funded by the International Planned Parenthood Federation (IPPF). The IPPF, the world's largest international network of private population policy organisations, is an exponent of the neo-Malthusian ideology, according to which the basic cause of underdevelopment is held to be not an unequal distribution of resources, but excessive population growth, above all within the poorer classes. Its Brazilian branch, BEMFAM, armed with the same ideology, operates in the main on the outskirts of towns and in rural areas in the Northeast. It exhorts poor women to fulfill their 'family planning duties' and encourages them to improve their standard of living by having fewer children.

BEMFAM started out in the 1970s by offering the pill free at its own clinics, although without suitable medical advice or care. In 1971 it was granted charitable status and has been able, as a result, to expand considerably its distribution network through contracts with the public health service, companies and other non-state organisations, and by taking on paid community workers.

BEMFAM regularly switches from one brand of pill to another, although these days, incidentally, the pills which it distributes are almost exclusively produced by the Schering subsidiary 'Berlimed'. It issues the pill to undernourished, older or ill women, and side-effects occur, such as nausea, headaches and irritability, which are the rule rather than the exception. BEMFAM rarely informs its patients about alternative methods of contraception.

The one exception to this rule was the coil, which many women had fitted in the early seventies without being given either information regarding the risks involved or proper medical check-ups before or after fitting. As a result of being fitted with these coils, some of which were still in the experimental stage, many women experienced complications including inflammation, heavy haemorrhaging and even unwanted pregnancies. The coil was consequently deemed unsuitable for use by BEMFAM as its main form of contraception.

Very little information is provided about safe forms of contraception for women, such as the diaphragm or the rhythm method. The use of condoms, although a well-known method of birth control, is unacceptable to most men, since they regard contraception as the woman's responsibility.

The World Health Organisation has estimated that for three to four million women per annum the only solution to an unwanted pregnancy is an illegal abortion carried out, in the majority of cases, under dangerous conditions. Poorer women, for example, often carry out their own abortions with the help of poisonous herbs, by injecting themselves with several one-month doses of hormonal contraceptives (available in almost every chemist's shop), by inserting pointed objects or probes or injecting acidic liquids into the womb. As a consequence, 200,000 women each year are taken into hosital after abortions with serious, sometimes fatal, complications.

'Faced with the nausea caused by taking hormones internally, with painful abortions, with marital rape, with having to bear sole responsibility for contraception and so on, many women regard sterilisation as the light at the end of the tunnel', writes the women's health organisation *SOS Corpo da Mulher*. The number of sterilisations carried out on women has increased dramatically since the mid-seventies, and sterilisation is now the most common form of contraception.

Sixty-six per cent of all married women or women living with a partner and aged between 15 and 49 use some form of contraception. Of these, 44 per cent have been sterilised and 41 per cent are on the pill. In states in the Northeast, the North and the Mid-West the proportion of women using contraception who have been sterilised is even higher (71 per cent in Goias, 61 per cent in Pernambuco).

Seventy per cent of Brazil's sterilised women have had the operation since 1980. They are always younger women (in 16 per cent of all cases, women under the age of 25), and in particular women living on the outskirts of towns, who normally have themselves sterilised as part of a caesarian section during the birth of a second or third child. Consequently, a world-record 31 per cent of all Brazilian babies are now born by caesarian section. In recent years the birth rate has fallen rapidly in every region of Brazil and in every social class, but especially in poor urban areas; between

1980 and 1984 alone it fell by 19 per cent, from an average of 4.3 to 3.5 children per woman.

The wave of sterilisations sweeping Brazil is supported by international organisations, primarily through training programmes for doctors. Seventy-five per cent of all sterilisations are carried out in the public health service. Sometimes doctors press their woman patients into having the operation on dubious grounds of medical necessity. As a rule, however, the operation is carried out illegally, that is, without there being any medical grounds at all, during a caesarian section carried out specifically for the purpose, and is often paid for by the woman herself at a price which is generally higher than the minimum wage.

The strength of many women's desire for sterilisation is illustrated by the practice — widespread particularly in the North and the Northeast for many years now — of politicians offering free sterilisations as vote winners during election campaigns. However, to what extent these sterilisations are 'voluntary', in other words based on the woman's independence of decision, has been questioned time and again by the women's health movement. Apart from the lack of alternative contraception available, there are many other pressures which drive women, often at an early age, to take so final a decision and which suggest that the rapid fall in the birth rate is actually the result of far-reaching social change.

Brazil's increasing urbanisation as a result of industrialisation and the concentration of land in fewer and fewer hands, as well as the shift away from subsistence farming towards paid labour, has reduced the importance to the family of child labour. What is more, many women say that given the economic crisis, constantly rising food prices and the increasing shortage of housing in the towns, they can no longer afford a lot of children. Many women also find it impossible to cope with both paid employment and child-care, a task which still falls entirely to them. Nursery schools are few and far between and even the traditional social network of the extended family and neighbours is rapidly disintegrating as migration and isolation increase.

The modern mass media has helped, especially through advertising and television series, to link the model nuclear family — two or three children — with the ability to consume. At the same time, there is a contradiction between Brazilian machismo, which requires women to be permanently available sexually, and Catholic morality and notions of virgin purity and respect for men, as a result of which the female body and female sexuality continue to be totally taboo.

Sterilisation is often seen as the most appropriate method of contraception. The decision to be sterilised is often a scientific solution to a serious crisis in a woman's personal life; however, the 'sexual freedom' and improved living conditions which sterilisation promises generally fail to materialise. Often the decision is bitterly regretted when the woman's desire for children reemerges later in life. Sterilisation as the expression of a crisis in society's view of the female role leaves many women in a vacuum: while making it impossible for them to gain recognition by society as mothers, the promise of self-fulfilment at work generally proves illusory because of unemployment and worsening working conditions.

Not until the late seventies, when feminists first dared to take a greater part alongside their then allies — the Church at grassroots level and comrades in left-wing political parties — in the struggle against the military dictatorship, were issues such as sexuality, contraception and abortion openly discussed in the women's movement. The women's groups spawned by the social movements in the urban slums also pressed for discussion of these everyday problems. Although the criticisms voiced by left-wingers and the Church at grassroots level about authoritarian birth control measures such as BEMFAM's were justified, these criticisms also led such groups to reject on principle the provision of all forms of contraception and of abortion, both of which they saw as 'imperialist attacks on the interests of the Brazilian people'. The women's movement in turn rejected this stance essentially in favour of a rise in the birth rate and based on conservative values — on the grounds that it was just as authoritarian over the decisions which women take about their own lives as BEMFAM's advocacy of birth control. The women's movement pointed out that it was precisely this laissez-faire approach which had enabled the private population policy organisations to become so powerful in the first place.

During the early eighties the Brazilian government began to reappraise its attitude to birth control. In doing so it was reacting on the one hand to the conditions set by the International Monetary Fund, which during negotiations for the rescheduling of Brazil's debt demanded that population policy measures be taken, and on the other hand to the pressure being exerted by the increasingly vocal and increasingly political women's movement. In 1983, despite the bitter opposition of the Catholic Church, the Ministry of Health adopted the Integrated Women's Health Programme

(PAISM). Having been formulated for the most part by feminists from the women's health movement, it essentially addressed women's demands for access to safe forms of contraception and extensive information about them. It did not address the abortion issue. During this period of political transition, in which the women's movement also gained access to state institutions in other areas, the Ministry of Health established an internal Commission for Reproductive Rights.

Since then, the women's movement's hopes for changes to Brazil's institutional framework have been bitterly disappointed. To date the PAISM has not been implemented. It has failed as a result both of a lack of interest on the part of those responsible for it and of the corruption within a health service which is incapable of meeting universally accepted standards, both in the public sector and in the large private sector for which it works under contract.

Women are still being forced to meet their requirements for contraception on the so-called free market controlled by the pharmaceutical industry, the doctors who carry out sterilisations and 'family planning organisations'. Brazil's privatised and commercialised population policy is established, and the ranks of those who implement it are swelling: since the mid-seventies some 200 private organisations like BEMFAM, most of which are funded from abroad and have similar programmes and objectives, have been set up. On the totally unregulated contraceptives market there has been a massive increase in recent years in the number of women using the dangerous one- and three-month hormonal injections Unociclo, Perlutal and Depo-provera, all of which are available without a prescription.

The women's health movement continues to fight, through campaigns and demonstrations on the streets of Brazil, for reproductive rights for women. The principal demands made during a four-month national campaign in 1989 which was fought under the slogan 'Women's health, a right we'll have to fight for' were firstly that the PAISM be implemented and secondly that companies be prosecuted if they demand proof of sterilisation before employing women.

In addition, delegates to the 10th National Women's Congress in September 1989 launched a campaign for the legalisation of abortion, which has in the past been legal only for the victims of rape or where the mother's life is in danger, and which is generally not guaranteed by the public health service even in cases such as these. The silence surrounding this taboo subject has to be broken so that it can be discussed openly both in and outside the women's movement.

That said, the women's health movement is not concerned solely with formal rights and the creation of a more woman-friendly social system. In recent years there has also been increasingly open discussion of sexuality. Cultural 'modernisation' and the breakdown of social cohesion in village and neighbourhood has led to an idealisation of sexual satisfaction, which, as a symbol of happiness, remains unattainable for women — especially given the sexual violence to which they are often subjected. 'We still have a lot to learn', says one *SOS Corpo da Mulher* worker 'before we will understand what this Brazilian mixture of sexism in all of society's spheres of influence and the marketing of an erotic sexuality on the one hand, and of the gloomy ethics of the Catholic Church, virgin purity and the taboos which surround the female body on the other hand, mean in terms of women's everyday experience of female sexuality.'

Susanne Schultz

'Laws by men have made inequalities out of differences'

In 1962 Brazilian women still enjoyed the same legal status as Indians, children and the mentally handicapped: without the permission of her husband a Brazilian woman could not legally sign contracts, work or buy on hire purchase. In the 30 years since then considerable progress has been made. The first step towards equal rights was the recognition of women as citizens, in other words the granting of women's suffrage. Women in Sweden gained the vote in 1862, those in Norway in 1913, in Denmark in 1915, in Holland in 1919 — in Brazil women were not legally entitled to vote until 1932. The campaign had lasted more than a decade, from its launch in 1921 by the legendary Bertha Lutz. The Brazilian League for the Advancement of Women, founded in 1922 was a coalition of positivist women from 'better circles' whose aim was to raise the level of women's education and to secure civil and political rights.

The political climate of the twenties, during which the struggle for women's suffrage and the women's movement in Brazil began, was one of great turbulence. Culturally the country was under the influence of the modernist movement, politically it was a time of massive anti-war protests, and socially the period was dominated by class struggle; strikes and general protests were the order of the day.

The feminist *O Nosso Jornal* (Our Newspaper), began in 1919 and launched a campaign to have women admitted to the civil service.

In 1927 the state of Rio Grande do Norte passed a law granting women unlimited suffrage. Hence in 1932, when universal female suffrage was introduced at national level, there were already elected women in office in this state, including Alzira Soriano, the mayor of Lages and incidentally the first woman ever to be elected to public office in South America.

The 1934 Constitutional Assembly, whose members included one women, incorporated a series of new guarantees into Brazilian labour law and laid down rules governing maternity leave and equal pay. The 1937 *Estado Novo* (New State) under Getulio Vargas, however, was a step in the wrong direction for women, since it seriously impeded their ability to exercise their newly-won civil rights.

In 1946 not a single woman was elected to Congress, although many deputies owed their election totally to the influence exerted and efforts made by women, in their areas and at election meetings. At this time the parties were really only interested in women as workers; even among the newly-elected deputies there were few who supported the struggle for women's emancipation.

By 1982 — when the military regime was on its last legs there were numerous women in elected office and in civil service posts. The 1986 elections to the Constitutional Assembly highlighted the advances which had been made; though not numerous, they were nevertheless significant. In the same year women farmworkers fighting for the right to join unions, for a woman's right to own property and to be recognised as the head of a family, held their first assembly.

In 1986 only 26, or five per cent, of the 559 people elected to the Constitutional Assembly were women. The women represent 16 of Brazil's 24 federal states. In general they tend to be on the left and progressive, yet the regional breakdown is not good, since the majority of them represent the less influential states. In addition, the regions which they represent are all at different states in their development and mobilisation. Of the 26, four were elected as a result of their husbands' influence, three because of the backing of their extended families, two are daughters of former presidents, three are members of left-wing parties and three are active feminists. At the same time, not a single woman was elected to the Senate, despite the fact that women make up half the population and half the electorate.

The results of the 1986 elections to the Constitutional Assembly also made it possible for women to force the incorporation of demands made as part of the UN Decade of Women into the constitution, and to compel Congress to draw up proper laws to implement them. However, because of Brazil's noted reluctance to prosecute offenders, the non-observance or circumventing of laws is commonplace, and constant supervision is required. The only way to ensure that it takes place is by grassroots mobilisation.

One change introduced by the new constitution overtly politicises an area which has previously been in the private domain. The term 'family' has been redefined to allow a (single) woman to be recognised as the head of her family. A further advance requires the state to take responsibility for children as citizens, a recognition of the social function of motherhood.

But there is only limited scope for women to make their presence felt in the Constitutional Assembly. An opinion poll conducted among female candidates revealed that many of them were standing for election at the request of parties and knew little about the structure of the Constitutional Assembly, its programmes or the motions which it debates. These female candidates did not identify, either ideologically or in terms of policy, with the parties they were representing. They were women who worked in the community, in the service sector, raising consciousness or giving careers advice. None of them was politically active and several of them were completely unprepared to assume the posts for which they were standing. Their relationship with the parties they were representing was more accidental than anything else.

Naturally, of the women standing, there were also some, like Benedita da Silva of the PT, who had proven track records in the social struggle and were militant in their outlook. Yet these women have not secured any important positions within the parties. Indeed, the parties treated their female candidates with total disregard, refusing to provide logistic and financial backing during the election campaign. In general women candidates were not assigned electoral areas of their own; they were placed in secondary positions on the party lists and their job was to use their influence to help male candidates nearer the top of the list win more votes. In other words, with few exceptions the nomination of women was not a sincere attempt to get them elected.

Although the majority of the female candidates were not committed to the aims of the Brazilian feminist movement, those who did identify with the movement's demands introduced into the debate the proposals contained in the Women's Charter. This charter was drawn up at the Women's Federal Assembly and demands:

1. a fixed percentage of the budget to be set aside for the building of crèches;
2. that women be treated with respect by forensic institutes, public prosecutors and defence lawyers;
3. the right to a non-stereotyped media image for women;
4. that motherhood be recognised as a social responsibility;
5. that Brazilian labour law be revised to cater for women's needs;
6. that the family be protected, even where there has been no marriage, and that women should have equal rights within relationships;
7. the right to give birth and to abortion;
8. the banning of dangerous drugs and experiments in the field of reproductive technology;
9. that companies be prevented from restricting their employment

of women to those who are attractive and under forty;

10. that it be made easier for single women to buy houses;

11. the promotion of political awareness and that women be encouraged to participate in political life.

The laws formulated by men have made inequalities out of differences. Whenever laws are being made, women must be there, must take advantage of their access to the decision-making process to fight for the recognition of their real value and to raise their status.

As one of the women talked to says, 'Without the presence of women, blacks, workers and peasants, the Constitutional Assembly will be conservative and right of centre.'

Loreley Garcia

Women and industrial action

During the nineteenth century woman workers in Brazil were first employed in large numbers in agriculture, industry and trade. Around this time Brazil also began to witness the emergence — in response to the social circumstances of the day — of a women's movement.

At the turn of the century Brazil's labour market was expanding as capitalism began to take root. In São Paulo, the first textile mills opened, mainly recruiting women and children from among the poor urban population. From the beginning the working conditions in these mills were unfit for human beings. Women and children lived in the mills, worked more than 16 hours a day, and slept and ate between the machines. Women earned half a man's wage, girls a quarter. Beatings and rapes were part of everyday life.

The conditions under which both men and women were forced to work were demoralising. Women were also subjected to physical attacks and abuse and paid less than their male colleagues.

As a result, working women began to take an active part in the various working class movements, although at first only in their general campaigns (for shorter working hours, improvements in working conditions, wage rises). Those who attempted to organise in trade unions or played a leading role in the struggle jeopardised their reputations, since a public life was not seen as suitable for women.

Despite the harsh living conditions which women workers endured — constantly exhausted as they juggled with housework and paid employment — they were not prepared to let anything stand in the way of their participation in the political struggle against injustice. They began their own struggle inside the anarchist and socialist movements.

Seamstresses employed by the ready-made clothing manufacturers expressed their demands and their unionisation plans in the anarchist newspaper *A Terra Livre* (Free Country). In a manifesto which appeared in this newspaper in 1906, they asked: 'What do these vultures pay us for so much effort? A miserable wage which defies description! Yet we also want leisure time, time for reading and learning; for our access to education is limited. And if that continues then our ignorance and lack of awareness will see to it that we are never anything more than human machines, machines which our greedy murderers can run as and when they wish. How can a person read a book when she goes to work at seven in the morning and doesn't come home until late at night, until after eleven?'

This was the first strike manifesto ever prepared by striking woman workers in Brazil. It was published in 1907 by the São Paulo seamstresses during the general strike which paralysed the city for a month. The workers demanded wage increases and an eight-hour-day. The general strike called on the 1st of May marked the climax of one of Brazil's earliest labour disputes, which had begun in 1905.

During the 1920s and early 1930s female weavers and seamstresses were active in the labour movement, organising countless strikes and publicly condemning their working conditions and miserable wages. By the late 1940s and 1950s women were well represented in the labour movement. Their activities were centered on São Paulo, where many were prosecuted for taking part in picketing.

In Brazil the 1950s was a period of intense industrialisation which resulted in enduring economic and social change. The proportion of women working in industry fell off, as the focus of women's employment shifted from production to the service sector.

Within the industrial sector, the remaining women began working in a wide variety of industries including metal, machine-building and the electrical appliance manufacturing industry. The textile industry — traditionally the branch of industry with the highest percentage of women workers — ceased to be the industrial sector's leading employer of women.

The increased employment of women in heavy industry was caused by Brazil's industrial expansion and growing urbanisation together with the wage-cutting policy adopted by the government after the military seized power in 1964. It was not only women's lives which changed, but also those of men and children. The economic situation forced everyone onto the labour market. In order to survive during this period of falling real wages, families had to acquire new habits and adopt structures which broke with tradition.

As employment levels rose, large numbers of women workers began to mobilise within the trade unions, which no longer restricted themselves to traditional demands, but instead launched a debate on the link between class exploitation and oppression on the grounds of sex. There were the first murmurings of a policy which acknowledged links between private oppression at home and the exploitation of women by men at work. At last people were becoming aware of the political significance of the home situation:

the family as the stronghold of men's oppression of women, not only through its ideologically repressive role, but also because it is the place where women work without pay and thereby facilitate the accumulation of capital. Gradually sections of the popular and trade union movements came together to discuss this whole question.

The first womens' trade union congresses took place during the late 1970s. In 1979 woman metalworkers organised two congresses, one in São Paulo and the other in São Bernardo do Campo, on the problems encountered by women at work.

These congresses came about as a result of the huge strikes organised by the metalworkers' union in the reglon, in particular in the industrial belt around São Paulo. The strikes were a response to the government's wage-cutting policy and developed into a major national movement opposed to state control of the trade union movement and the military government.

Women played a major part in the strikes — as strikers themselves and also as the wives of striking metalworkers and as members of the popular movements, whose support was crucial.

Their participation prompted the women metalworkers to organise regular meetings for working women at which women's issues could be discussed. They realised that it was not considered important, either in the family or by society, for women to receive vocational training. This and other deeply rooted prejudices led to women earning less than men, even when doing a job of equal value. Since the law on equal pay is often circumented by employers on the grounds that women are not as highly qualified as men, women often feel forced to do overtime.

These considerations, along with dangerous and unhygienic working conditions, moved the women to compile a list of demands. Their major goals were the abolition of overtime, the introduction of crèches, the 40-hour-week and paid leave for mothers taking children to the doctor. Women's work and health was a further focus of attention. The lack of medical care provided and repressive methods employed by the government's birth control programme were strongly condemned.

As women became increasingly active in social processes and trade union activities in the 1980s, women's issues became an official area of activity within the trade union movement. For the first time ever the experiences of women from various spheres (the unions, the popular movements, the women's movement) were pooled and analysed, and strengthened their standing in the trade union movement.

Meanwhile the founding of the new trade union umbrella organisation, the CUT, marked the trade union movement's newly-won independence from the state. Encouraged by the unions' increased interest, women made vigorous efforts to have their concerns taken seriously in this newly-created organisation. At the CUT's national advisory council women trade unionists put down a motion calling for the establishment of a 'Commission for Women's Issues' (CNQMT), which was agreed in 1986. The commission would tackle basic issues including:

— the situation of women on the Brazilian labour market, for although there are now considerable numbers of them their jobs are largely restricted to the lowest earnings band,
— the plight of women farmworkers,
— suggestions that the CUT, as the leading body in the working-class struggle, should also take over the role of organising on women's issues with the aim of increasing the participation of working women and of representing their particular interests.

Despite the difficulties which the CNQMT encountered, women trade unionists believe there is considerable progress. Women's issues have at last been incorporated into the CUT's programme.

In 1988 the CNQMT organised the first national conference on women's issues, a hugely important event which succeeded in winning the support of the congress of the CUT, anything but a machismo-free organisation, and in gathering together unionised female office staff and workers from all over Brazil.

There is still a great deal to do if woman workers are to become involved more actively and effectively in the various organisations, in the labour market and in the trade unions and are to pursue with any degree of success the demands of working women. Four out of every ten of Brazil's workers are women. The CUT must not allow them to be sidelined in the battle being fought by their class.

According to the CNQMT: 'The inequalities and the problems imposed specifically on women are an intensified form of the oppression and exploitation to which the entire working class is subjected. As such the unionisation of women is a job for the working class and does not mean division, but rather a strengthening and unifying force in the struggle against the bourgeois ruling class.'

Maria Cecília Camargo

Women's Organisations

The Cabo women's centre

Many women in Brazil find out about the women's centre in Cabo through the women's calendar which they have published for several years. Cabo is a small town on the outskirts of Recife and between 1958 and 1964 was one of the rural opposition movement's strongholds. In 1978 a huge strike in Brazil's sugar-cane producing region, which along with the strikes in São Paulo marked the beginning of open opposition to the military dictatorship, was organised from there.

Efigenia Maria is the president of the Cabo women's centre:

'It all started in 1978, when women belonging to one of the local organisations got together to form a women's group. The following year, the women organised a celebration for the 8th of March and arranged to continue meeting after the celebrations and to campaign for water, electricity and drainage in their area. They also decided to get together to build small houses for their families.

The women wouldn't let go and soon got down to work, but the men kept sticking their noses in whenever there was anything to be decided. The women didn't like it and wanted to become more independent.

So someone suggested that we should set up our own women's centre. The groups in the various areas of the town would continue to exist and the centre would be somewhere where we could swap experiences. One representative from each group was to come to a monthly information meeting, and every three months the women would together evaluate the centre's work. The aim was for as many women as possible to get involved, to take part in and influence the work — and that there should be very little influence exerted from outside. That's why we wanted to be independent both of the churches and the local groups. On 25 May 1984 600 women celebrated the opening of the women's centre.

Our health work is very important, because there isn't a single maternity home in the entire district which is open to all women. So a lot of women die each year. At the centre we regularly carry out examinations, including those designed to detect cancer. A woman lawyer advises and accompanies the women if they have legal problems, in particular in the family and at work.

On the first floor we have a number of rooms where women can attend dressmaking courses or learn various handicrafts to make things for their families or for sale in the centre's shop. Initiatives include a crèche, a building suitable for larger meetings and our work with women's groups in the small villages around Cabo, where we talk to the women about health matters and family planning. We also try to grow vegetables and medicinal herbs together and to raise fish, shrimps, pigs and chickens. In that way we hope to extend their usual diet of flour and rice. What's more, the women can sell anything that's left over at a fair price in their own villages.

All the same it was a year before the women were ready to have a go at planting a garden and selling part of their crop. Never before in their entire lives had they been "masters" of something, never before had they had anything to sell. They thought no one would take them seriously if they wanted to sell something. That everyone would laugh at them.

Our biggest problem at the women's centre at the moment is that although we've gained more and more members over the last few years — we now have more than 5,000 — only a few of them take part in the regular work. So at the moment we're not taking any new members. First we want to evaluate our work to date.

In families where the people are still living together as a family, they're normally all — man, woman and children — employed in the sugar-cane industry for six months of the year, although it's the man who gets the money. Today most sugar-cane workers live on the outskirts of towns and not near the sugar-cane refineries as they used to. You see, they'd fought for the right to two hectares of land per family, so that they could grow food, so many refinery owners drove all their workers off the land and into the towns. Nowadays the lorries drive to the poor suburbs of the towns at six in the morning and choose those who are going to be "allowed" to work that day. That way they also make it difficult for the workers to organise.

For the rest of the time, when they're not harvesting sugar-cane, there's no regular work. The men sometimes look for casual work. A lot of them drink huge quantities of sugar-cane liquor and start beating their wives and children.

The women have to see to it that the family survives, see to the food and the children. There's often trouble if a woman wants to get together with other women. The men like their wives to stay at home to do the washing and look after the kids. They say, "The women's centre is dreadful, a gang of communists who just want to destroy families." But the women say they've become more competent and more self-confident because of the centre and now know more about their rights.

We get some of our money from abroad, for example from *Terre des hommes*. The local authority pays the centre's two women doctors and a woman driver. One of our problems is that recently the government has begun to want more and more control over the funds of institutions for which it's not directly responsible. Another problem is that the government often agrees to the demands made by the popular movements, but then it has to be pushed into giving just a few families land for houses, let alone the whole group, as it promised. That cripples many movements. The government printed fantastic leaflets setting out women's demands, but it didn't take any of them on board.

Our work concentrates on women first of all, because women make up the majority of the population. Secondly, because they have a lot of energy and important experiences to contribute. Thirdly, it's vital that women's issues are part of any political debate. What's more, the way women treat each other changes as a result of their humaneness. I think it's very important that women from the working class fight for change within their own families, even if that means a lot of grief and a lot of rows.

For example, the women here are trying to be more careful about family planning. Their husbands generally refuse to have anything to do with it, and many women take the pill without having anything explained to them by the doctor or allow themselves to be talked into being sterilised. Even girls as young as 18! When we conducted a survey at the centre it turned out that more than half of the women here have been sterilised. Also, far too many women die from infections resulting from secret abortions.

For me it's not a question of who's for and who against abortion, but of who has the opportunity to have children. If a girl of 14 has an illegitimate child, she's often thrown out by her family and ends up as a prostitute. It often takes three years for maintenance to be sorted out in a paternity suit in the courts. A lot of women give up before then.

Many people have difficulty even imagining that things could be different. Many just say, "It's God's will, so we can't change it." Or, "He who suffers in this life, will have a better life after death." The Church is very powerful here. There are some priests and vicars who forbid women to take part in our meetings. It's very important that we combat this authoritarianism and encourage women to become more confident and make their own decisions. But every day it gets more difficult to believe that things will ever be different, more... just, more humane. On the other hand, what will our children's world be like if we don't resist today? I can't live without a dream.

Today, unlike during the military dictatorship, we can say whatever we like, but it doesn't make much difference. Speaking the truth is fast becoming a luxury, because it doesn't help. The television tells people what to think. Poor women dream of living like the beautiful, rich, white wives of the industrialists in TV series. We have to have confidence in ourselves, hope and also patience with ourselves. Meeting other women and other groups gives us courage because we can see that there are others who think like we do and share our dreams.'

Interview by Gerdi Nützel

Who are Brazil's feminists?

The lift attendant lets me out on the fourth floor of an old high-rise office block. Right in the middle of Rio, I am about to attend my first meeting with Brazilian feminists. About twenty doors, all looking the same. No signs to reveal whether I'll find an export firm, a lawyer's office, a woman dentist's practice or even the women's meeting place for which I'm searching. Room 408, that must be it! In this country, which otherwise prizes the personal touch so highly, you have no chance without a room or apartment number.

Tharís, whom I know only from the telephone, greets me warmly. During a short trip to Hamburg she discovered that I was interested in organising an exchange with feminists in Brazil and also in bringing with me a series of slides (on the theme 'Hamburg women on the move'.) It was she who offered to organise a meeting.

We sit down at a large table which fills roughly a quarter of the room. Before anything else, I am required to pass judgement on this table, since it and the five chairs around it are the first things to be acquired by the women for their new room, which is to be formally inaugurated here and now in my presence. I am moved and at the same time ashamed. While woman friends in Germany have a whole floor, with a cafe, for their project, this room is occupied by three women's projects.

But this is no time for sentimentality. Together we set up the slide projector and attempt to darken the room. It's midday and it proves impossible to block out the sun entirely with the curtains hanging at the windows. I get a little nervous, especially when Thaís suggests that after a short introduction from her it might be best if I introduce myself. Although after two holidays in Brazil I'm able to make myself understood fairly well, speaking in public off the top of my head... oh, God! In fact, she later came to my aid.

In the meantime the first women arrive. There are hugs, kisses, an excited exchange of news; the room vibrates. My first impression is that these are mature women, aged between 35 and 45. I'm very curious. As the women arrive in dribs and drabs during their lunch breaks, a typical German-Brazilian conflict of interests arises: thinking ahead to the end of the lunch break (officially an hour, but extendable with *jeito* to one and a half or two hours), I remark that we should begin if we are to get through our programme; Thaís, on the other hand, is thinking of many who might still come and doesn't want them to miss the beginning. After half an hour we finally make a start.

Today is a special day, says Thaís, the day of *Nossa Senhora da Conceiçao*, whom the Brazilians identify with Mary in the Catholic tradition and with Iemanja, the sea-goddess, in the Afro-Brazilian. Everyone regards this as a good omen for the future of the women's room.

Next I introduce myself, talk about my passions, that for feminism and that for Brazil, and of how happy I am to be able to combine the two today. The women are in a talkative mood and in good old women's group tradition, they all proceed to introduce themselves.

Maria Lucia, a 42-year-old actress — 'my life is a mixture of disarray and the red flag' — is now heavily into psychodrama and working as a therapist. She gave up her career in the theatre more than ten years ago to work in women's street theatre: 'Now I see to it that others make a scene.' The others of whom she speaks are female friends in the movement, as well as women from the poor areas of the town. They write and perform bitter-sweet plays about the everyday lives of Brazilian women; they mix abortive drug cocktails outside chemists shops, accusing the owners of treating women's health irresponsibly, in community halls they perform the *missa femea*, a women's mass which by using original elements of the liturgy ironically denounces the Church's oppression of women. Maria Lucia and her friends have also written a satirical novel, a feminist biography covering the period from the fifties to the present day. Maria Lucia lives with her 12-year-old daughter, who's already following in her mum's footsteps. Last year she couldn't be talked out of leading, on roller-skates and carrying a banner, a demonstration to open a women's congress.

Solange, the 38-year-old (single) mother of an 8-year-old boy, says of herself, 'I do everything, and what thanks do I get?' In addition to having once worked in the Brazilian parliament, she has worked for *SOS Racismo*, and one of the many women's projects in which she's been involved was an investigation into the sale of dangerous abortive drugs, which subsequently led her into other work on public opinion. She too loves to act. At the moment this trained anthropologist is trying to discover the origins of old children's games and childhood legends. Curiosity and her involvement in politics have also taken her to Angra dos Reis. Together with the people living near this German-built nuclear power station she's gathering routine knowledge and details of the risks of radiation damage which it poses, and which Brazilian society prefers to suppress. Although the patriarchal university by which she's employed guarantees her enough for a basic existence, her benefits don't go much beyond maternity cover, despite her popularity with the students. 'So as not to go crazy', she sews all her feelings into beautiful patchwork quilts. It's a hobby which proves useful whenever she finds herself in serious financial difficulty.

Branca, 50 years old, two children, fondly dubbed by the others 'our president', learned her politics from the factory work campaigns organised by the radicals of 1968 and witnessed the rise of Brazilian feminism while in the US. After the demise of the dictatorship, she fought — in her capacity as Rio's president of the National Women's Council — for women's rights to be guaranteed in the new Brazilian constitution. 'It's my ambition', she says, 'to fight an official political campaign from a feminist standpoint.'

Hildesia, the mother of four grown-up children and a black woman trade unionist, has for years been fighting machismo in her union. Women's committees are a tangible success, but she doesn't want herself and women to be marginalised by them. This trained teacher not only teaches history, she is also making it and putting it down on paper at the same time. Her latest work is a women's calendar.

Giselle, a doctor who has worked in the *favelas* for the last 12 years, and also from time to time for the Ministry of Health. Because of the critical stance which she's adopted over women's health and family planning she is now unemployed. Along with the others, this single mother is planning to organise an international conference on population policy and genetic technology.

Joselina, one of the organisers of the First National Congress of Black Women, works as a teacher during the day and in the evenings shares her knowledge of English with her black sisters and represents women's interests in the Black Movement and on women's committees in the poor suburbs. She's the only woman present who lives in the Baixada Fluminense, a huge suburb two hours' bus journey from the centre of Rio. Her desire to establish a women's centre there involves her in a great deal of painstaking work. 'It'll be women who change the city,' she maintains, 'Even if they are still denying their female identities at the moment.' Despite all her work, Jo never misses an opportunity to have a beer with her friends or to go dancing.

Madalena, a woman in her mid-forties with a daughter at university in London, she is a committed radio journalist, who, with

Thaís, founded the women's radio station *Fala Mulher* (Speak, woman). Previously with *SOS Mulher*, she is a long-time member of the PT, where she established the first women's section. Now, in the middle of the campaign to elect PT candidate Lula, she is everywhere and nowhere, her lilac flag always to hand.

Thaís, 33 years old and living alone, uses journalism to bring together women throughout Brazil and the world: 'An article can sometimes achieve more than thirty pages of research into women's issues.' She works both with REDEH, a network on women's health and reproductive rights, and with Cemina, an information and advice centre for women's groups. Her active opposition to genetic policy and support for ecological issues leave her little time for a private life. Yet despite a lack of cycle tracks and the hectic traffic, she spends precious time each day cycling across the Moloch of Rio.

What a variety! The room is full of lived experience. Bottles of beer, dried cod balls and shrimp patties are passed around alternately. How simple it is here to combine the personal with the political. That was our slogan in Germany, yet it's hard for me to imagine a comparable situation back home: woman trade unionists, independent feminists, social democrats, lesbians, Afro-Germans and Greens together in one room enjoying an exchange of views. I am overwhelmed, but hardly surprised, when the door opens and a man enters, only to be greeted warmly rather than thrown out. The women notice my reserve and introduce Guido to me as a feminist and ecologist involved in the struggle to save the Amazon. His friendly unobtrusiveness makes it easier for me to set aside the principle that woman's meetings should be women-only.

I show my slides: 'Hamburg women on the move'. Although their content is so alien, they're well received; there's a great deal of laughter, and the women all talk at once. Those aspects which divide German and Brazilian women are taken in good humour.

How would our women's movement look if we could do that too?

Petra Sorge

Not one, but many

The Brazilian women's movement is diverse. It reflects the heterogeneity of women's living conditions in a society marked by huge regional and structual differences, but above all by extreme social inequalities.

Whilst women in the relatively economically privileged middle classes concentrate their energies within the feminist movement on attaining a modern standard of living with opportunities for personal, material and cultural development; the women of the *povo* organise in the towns and in the countryside above all in order to satisfy their basic needs; food, work, health care and somewhere to live.

Brazil's women's movement emerged in the 1970s as part of the population's opposition to the military dictatorship. (I will not attempt to go in detail into the longer tradition of feminist organisation and the participation of women in social struggles here.) When this difficult period of repression came to an end, and Brazil's economic crisis weakened the military, people found there was suddenly more scope for organising opposition and social movements. It was then that women started to speak for themselves. 1975, named International Women's Year by the UN, provided the impetus and focus.

Essentially the women's movement had its roots in two different soils: the first was the feminist movement, made up of middle-class women living in the large cities, many of whom were associated with left-wing political parties. These women established their own women's groups and used the publicity surrounding the 'International Women's Year' to promote debate and action. They began by finding premises of their own and organising their own publicity material: they launched magazines, opened women's centres and organised celebrations for the 8th of March. Opposition to the military regime was central. Nevertheless, there was some disagreement as to whether the movement should take part in the wider political struggle or whether its priority should be autonomy. The women in this movement organised the Women for Amnesty campaign, which in 1979 won its battle for an amnesty for all those who had been persecuted for political reasons.

The other root of the women's movement was among the poor women in the towns and on the land, who organised in the popular movements, in neighbourhood groups, in local groups, in opposition trade union groups and in their parishes as a direct response to their constantly worsening living conditions. Progressive forces within the Catholic Church did a great deal to support the population in its attempts to organise at grassroots level. To a large extent it was women who became involved, in the popular movements, local groups, mothers' clubs and so on.

The tradition of mothers' clubs goes back a long way and is an established part of the Catholic Church's traditional work with women. Just as base Christian communities have gradually become more political, so the character of many mothers' clubs has altered too. During the military period women from these groups led the 'campaign against increases in the cost of living', mobilised women in many urban areas and organised the huge 'empty pot' demonstrations.

Initially the diversity of priorities and tendencies within the women's movement took a back seat; shared opposition to the military dictatorship and political repression was paramount.

In 1978, São Paulo feminist groups organised the first large women's congress in which 500 women took part. This was followed in 1980 by a second congress with 4,000 participants, 1,300 of them women from the popular movements. Mobilisation on this scale generated enough publicity to provide sufficient protection for opposition demonstrations against the dictatorship to go ahead. The principal demands made by the first congress related to women and work (the right to employment, the struggle against discrimination, for example, in areas such as employment opportunities, earnings, pregnancy tests), the establishment of free crèches, the right to organise freely and to freedom of expression, a comprehensive, unrestricted amnesty, and across-the-board equality with men under criminal, civil and commercial law. The second congress discussed gender-motivated inequalities in the way children are educated, sexuality, abortion and family planning, violence against women, and the role of women in political organisations.

As the period of dictatorship drew to a close during the early eighties, maintaining a broad alliance opposed to the military regime ceased to be a priority. It became possible for women to turn their attention more specifically to women's issues. In the process the women's movement shifted away from the issues which had united it, and the diversity of opinion and priorities within its ranks became more apparent. The issues which divided the women in the feminist movement from those belonging to the popular movements, such as abortion and the woman's role, were no longer pushed aside.

Plans to set up a unified national women's organisation faded. The opposition movement's disintegration into different political parties (the PMDB, the PDT and the PT), which first became evident during the 1982 parliamentary and governors elections, also had an effect. The various factions within the women's movement aligned themselves with competing political parties (essentially the PMDB, favoured by the orthodox communist parties and old left-wing groupings, and the PT, the party of the new grassroots movements). Despite working for different parties in the election campaign, the women nevertheless managed to issue a joint feminist election appeal covering all the major demands of recent years to every party.

For the women's movement this loss of unity meant not only an ideological schism, but also increasing specialisation in and concentration on specific issues and projects, and thus an extension of its diversity into practical areas. In several towns including São Paulo, Porto Alegre, Rio and Recife, emergency groups (*SOS-Mulher*) and 'committees against violence' were established. Elsewhere groups and women's centres were set up to promote self-help and to offer counselling or medical advice on issues such as health, sexuality and reproduction. Research into women's issues at universities increased and more and more women's information centres opened. Political congresses, like the Bertha Lutz Tribunal — whose aim was to combat discrimination against women at work — and the Festival of Women in Art, were organised. In 1983 the OAM, an autonomous women's rights organisation, was set up in São Paulo.

The women belonging to the popular movements have also pursued their demands through women's groups. Mothers' clubs fight tenaciously for the redevelopment of their areas, for health centres and nursery schools. Autonomous women's associations have been set up independendtly of the Church, while meeting places and women's centres which run educational and handicraft courses and which house 'peoples' pharmacies' and sewing cooperatives have opened. Self-help and the struggle for more rights go hand in hand.

Although the two halves of the women's movement remain distinct, there has been a move towards practical co-operation in recent times: women from the feminist movements have become involved to some extent in urban areas and have helped the women from the popular movements to put together independent women's projects, such as women's centres, health groups, or campaigns like the one for 'cheap basic foodstuffs for our area'.

The women's network, *Rede Mulher*, founded in 1983 has also encouraged practical cooperation between the various women's groups and in this way taken advantage of the diversity which exists between them. One important point of shared interest is the activities organised annually for the 8th of March, a date which unites all the groups.

The women's movement has also extended its scope in that women now take part in the day-to-day running of a variety of what might loosely be termed 'pressure groups', including parties, free trade unions, associations, etc, and are thus able to pursue their own particular demands in those settings. Women's congresses have been organised by women members of the farmworkers' union CONTAG, by the CUT, and by the political parties. Women's committees have been established in the CUT and the PT. In addition, a growing number of women have been elected as deputies, mayors, or presidents of their trade unions, though it must be said that the percentage remains small.

When those sections of the old opposition movement which are now part of the PMDB began to form governments in various states and at national level after 1982, and in particular after 1986, a section of the women's movement also gained access to the decision-making process. In 1983 the women successfully pushed for the establishment of the first ever state-run equal opportunities offices in the states of São Paulo and Minais Gerais, and in 1985 for the setting up of the National Council for Women's Rights.

Although the resources available to and scope of these offices — and thus their influence — is relatively limited, their establishment nevertheless meant that the demands of the women's movement were recognised as legitimate demands. In addition, it meant that these demands would in future be given more weight within state structures. Numerous initiatives, including the establishment of 'women's police stations' in several states, should be seen in this light. However, the direct incorporation of state-run equal opportunities offices into the government apparatus also means dependence; the scope of the National Council for Women's Rights was drastically restricted under the Sarney Government, then the Collor government replaced its original team of highly-respected women's rights activists.

Having opened out and organised at various levels and in different areas of society, the Brazilian women's movement, which in the autumn of 1989 held its 10th national conference, today has many faces. Over the last few years it has conquered the public domain, particularly with the debate begun in 1986 on the new constitution. And in 1989, during Brazil's first free presidential elections, its members called upon all the candidates to reveal their policies on women's issues.

Cordula Stucke

Am I a feminist?

There isn't only one feminism, just as there isn't only one Brazil.

Feminism means ideas on the move.

Feminism is a revolutionary thing.

Feminism means opposing the machismo in society.

Feminism is a state of being.

Feminism causes divisions, in the family and at school, at work, in thought and in life.

Feminism is a part of the whole struggle.

Feminism requires one's whole body.

Feminism means thinking of oneself.

Feminism is more than socialism.

Feminism is a hackneyed term which hampers our work.

Feminism means feeling comfortable with one's sexuality.

Feminism is the disintegration of male and female roles.

Feminism is pride in being at women.

Feminism means being able to look others in the eye.

Feminism is the same as machismo; they're two extremes.

Feminism is not just an organised movement, it's also part of daily life, of work. Of everything that women are part of.

Feminism isn't a formula or recipe, it's building every day.

Feminism is an outlook on life.

Feminism is something that comes from inside.

Feminism is the need to emancipate something.

Feminism means walking side by side with men and not in front or behind them.

Feminism is underground work, secret work.

Feminism is a movement which takes in everything: the intellect, politics, sexuality and health.

Feminism makes whole people out of devalued women.

Feminism is more comprehensive than 'the women's movement'.

Feminism means not being frightened of change.

Feminism has always existed, but it's only now that the term is taking hold.

Feminism means finding oneself in the story of other women's lives.

Feminism is a step in the direction of change.

A selection of views from the 9th Federal Feminist Congress, São Bernardo do Campo Women's Committee

'We want more!'
International Women's Day

It is the afternoon of the 8th of March 1989, in the centre of São Paulo. The streets are full of women celebrating 'their day' Many of them have brightly-painted faces and lilac-coloured paper flowers in their hair. Placards remind us of the women textile workers who, a hundred years ago, were burned to death during a strike. There are loud condemnations of the incumbent president and calls for a general strike in the coming weeks. Many passers-by clutch at leaflets which detail the demands made by various women's groups for the 8th of March. Women trade unionists, women from the Workers' Party, women from the amnesty movement, women from a health centre, lesbians, woman teachers with their female pupils, all are on the streets together, singing and celebrating, protesting and challenging.

The huge variety of women present is also emphasised in their International Women's Day song, which they strike up over and over again, beating time on their flag-poles with saucepans:

We're on the streets this 8th of March.
With all women everywhere
We have no crèches for our children.
We earn less than the price of bread.
 We are women.
 We are important.
 We are not stupid.
No more will we look on while women are murdered.
No more will we look on while Indian women are exterminated.
And black women discriminated against.
And prostitutes beaten.
Our bodies are our own.
Legalise abortion.

In São Paulo preparations began well ahead of the 8th of March, with representatives of local groups and base Christian communities getting together. On the weekend before, there was a show with sketches and pantomime on the central square in St André, one of São Paulo's satellite towns. Each group had prepared its contribution, on family life, on what happens to women at job interviews and so on. A long discussion had developed on the slogan to be printed on T-shirts to advertise and finance this year's

International Women's Day campaign. Finally the women agreed on the words 'We want more...!'

This slogan was also printed in bold lettering on the leaflets handed out at the suburban railway station to the tired people streaming past on their way to work at five o'clock in the morning. Some started to read straight away, other leaflets floated immediately to the ground. While the women distributed the leaflets they discussed what they had done so far in their groups for the 8th of March.

The film 'Land for Rosa' made a powerful impression in many mothers' clubs. It is about a young woman who, heavily pregnant and with two children in tow, has joined a land occupation. There she experiences at first hand the contradiction between the politicians' promises and the brutal attacks carried out by the police, and eventually dies as a result. Some of the women from local groups were deeply affected by the film and prompted to consider how they could be more daring in their activities. Some arranged to go together to the closing demonstration on the 8th in the centre of São Paulo.

At the end of the demonstration São Paulo's mayor, Erundina, speaks in front of many, many women and not a few men. She says she is there as a working-class woman and citizen, as a former migrant from the Northeast, as a woman who shares many of their problems and wants improvements. Two Indian women climb up onto the platform and complain that men searching for mineral resources in the Amazonas region often attack and rape their daughters, some as young as ten. The women in the square protest loudly and once again shout out their demands: 'We want more...! Respect, freedom, health care, 120 days maternity leave, fair pay, crèches for our children.'

Gerdi Nützel

Rede Mulher — the women's network

How, in a country the size of Brazil, can women's groups make contact with and support each other when they are thousands of kilometers apart and have hardly any money? *Rede Mulher*, the women's network founded in the eighties by women's rights activists in São Paulo, aims to overcome these difficulties and to make other social movements aware of women's issues.

When *Rede Mulher* was founded, Moema Viezzer, the organisation's present leader, brought to it the experience of women's educational work which she had gleaned in exile in other Latin American countries. Of the name *Rede* she says, 'A network is like a fishing net, which is much stronger and more serviceable than a line. There are many knots, or intersections, but no hierarchy. *Rede Mulher* is aiming to be a kind of intersection at which Brazilian women's groups can meet'.

At first the network's activities involved only a few women in São Paulo. They managed to rent a small house to use as an office and won backing from the Latin American Council for Adult Education. But in order to get a clear idea of what the planned network of women's groups might look like, they needed to learn about existing women's groups and their links with other social movements. *Rede Mulher* therefore launched two surveys in São Paulo. In the first, women workers were asked about their links with the unions and their experience of union activity. The second survey dealt with the history and current importance of the mothers' clubs.

The studies involved information and discussion meetings, and the results were made available to the women who had taken part through a variety of publications. 'What kind of history is that?', is the title of a pamphlet which documents the formation of the mothers' clubs and their history from the second half of the dictatorship to the present day.

'The mothers' clubs were the "mothers" of many local groups', said one of the women who took part in the survey. They were largely established in Catholic communities, and only a small proportion were formed inside other organisations, for example, in political parties. 'Let me tell you a bit about what our mothers' clubs meetings were like then', said another of the participants. 'At the beginning of each meeting we would knit and crochet. Then we read from the Bible and considered what the content might have to do with our everyday lives. That was something new for us. We were a group of lay people reading the Gospel without priests or nuns. That was how it started; today when we read the Gospel we start with the problems in our area. Then the women began to demand a water supply, a sewage system, health centres and nursery schools, and through these small battles we began to see things differently and to see through things better.'

The high point of the mothers' clubs' activities was their 'campaign against increases in the cost of living', in which many other groups and organisations also took part. The campaign began in 1972 with a letter to those officials responsible for prices drawing their attention to the fact that rises in the price of basic goods seemed unstoppable. Three years later the mothers' clubs launched a survey on the cost of living in more than 2,000 households. In the process the movement grew: signatures were collected, public meetings held, meetings of the representatives of various local groups organised. They demanded that the government freeze the prices of essential goods, adjust wages in line with rises in the cost of living and more besides.

The campaign reached its peak in August 1978 with a public rally attended by 20,000 people in São Paulo's Praça da Sé, the town's best-known spot for public assemblies and demonstrations. At this rally a petition with around 1,300,000 signatures was to be presented to those responsible for prices. They failed to show up. Instead the police came and broke up the rally.

That September a delegation representing the campaign travelled to Brasilia to present the petition to the President of the Republic. It was turned away.

The women did not give up, but organised in a decentralised way throughout São Paulo and Campinas, drawing attention to their desperate plight with a number of meeting and actions which became known as 'empty pot' demonstrations.

In São Paulo the hardship that they shared had prompted a certain amount of co-operation between mothers' clubs and other groups well before *Rede Mulher* appeared on the scene.

The research carried out by *Rede Mulher* revealed that some mothers' clubs were now beginning to tackle issues which were specifically women's issues: 'We also discuss our everyday lives as women.'

The two surveys raised numerous points, both methodological and content-related, which the organisation was subsequently able to follow up in its work. Methodologically, the surveys had taken a form which *Rede Mulher* describes as an 'activating poll', since questions are designed not only to gather information, but at the same time also to prompt those surveyed to reflect and take action. The responses themselves revealed that many mothers' clubs had developed in parallel and had been able to enrich each other by sharing their experiences. It also emerged that there was still a lot of work to be done before women would be able to participate on equal terms in trade union activities.

Although the two surveys were limited to the São Paulo area, *Rede Mulher*'s aim was to link women's groups nationwide. In November 1975, in order to bring together representatives of rural and urban women's groups from all over Brazil, *Rede Mulher* organised the first Women's Education Workshop. Seventy-five women from 22 federal states took part. There was a wide variety of groupings: housewives, domestic servants, prostitutes, washerwomen... A poem written by one of the participants was taken as a starting point in order to prompt the women to tell their own stories of misfortune and activism and to reflect on the structural causes of inequality:

I am a woman, a Brazilian woman
and I suffer too
but I'm still fighting
for the right to live.

The women discovered that racism, the machismo which is widespread even in the social movements, and their lack of education, all help to keep them in a subordinate position. As a way of channelling their desire for joint action into something practical, they launched an initiative aimed at getting women's rights incorporated into the new Brazilian constitution.

Gradually more than 750 women's groups were drawn into the discussion process; their objective to formulate a series of demands for consideration by the Constitutional Assembly. With the help of lawyers, male and female, the groups produced list of demands in the form of a petition which was then signed by a total of 47,000 women in a nation-wide action.

This initiative and the campaign fought by the CNDM, the National Women's Council in Brasilia, were arguably the most important contributions made by women to the debate on the new constitution.

The constitution is now in place, yet the work goes on; in fact, it is more necessary than ever. *Rede Mulher* workers now run educational courses at federal state level on the subject of women's rights. The courses are attended by delegates from women's groups who then pass on their newly-acquired knowledge to their groups.

Today *Rede Mulher*, through its 13 full-time workers, provides further education for women and helps women's groups to make and maintain contact with each other. The network stays in touch with many of the groups by letter. It runs a lending library and its newspaper, *Cunhary*, which has been published at least twice yearly since March 1988, enables the groups — including some in neighbouring Latin American countries — to stay in touch with each other and to exchange information on women's problems and activities. *Rede Mulher* hopes to consolidate its work in this area through its own radio transmissions.

Conducting activating polls, organising educational workshops and facilitating communication are all important areas of *Rede Mulher*'s work. Theatre is also playing an increasingly signficant part. One play written and produced by women came about as a by-product of the mothers' club survey and led to the formation of a permanent women's theatre group. In 1988 the first ever national Women's Theatre Workshop took place, at which Augusto Boal, among others, introduced the women taking part to the methods employed in his 'Theatre of the Oppressed'.

Doris Jäger

Women and Solidarity

Rede Mulher
International links

Rede Mulher's work with women's organisations at international level, in which not only the organisation's own staff, but also women from the *favelas* and from rural areas are increasingly taking part, is also providing fresh impetus.

In Germany, for example, a delegation from *Rede Mulher* was able to learn about the work of 17 different women's organisations, such as Pro Familia, the International Women's Day of Prayer group and the IAF, the group which represents the interests of women married to foreigners. Some German organisations fund *Rede Mulher* projects. In an interview conducted at the end of 1989, Moema Viezzer expressed the hope that additional backing would soon allow *Rede Mulher* to move to a larger building with seminar rooms.

Yet financial support is, in her opinion, only one aspect of international solidarity. She considers it vitally important that women should be able to exchange views at grassroots level. 'We had the Goiania nuclear accident here', she explained during the interview, 'and not until I heard the reactions of women in Germany did I realise how many women's groups there are which oppose nuclear energy. Brazilian women have no idea what German women discuss at grassroots level. I'd consider it productive if women from action groups here and in Germany were able to exchange views on issues which perhaps have identical or similar causes in both countries. Because as a result of the international division of labour our worlds have for a long time been linked. You can see that, for example, from the fact that we get money from Germany, some of it from organisations which in turn get their funds from the government, when at the same time that very government has now extended its agreement with Brazil for building nuclear power stations. Another example is the foreign debt, although it will be some time before we can identify more clearly those areas of dependence which cause misery not just here but also in the "First World". I think that international solidarity between women needs to take an altogether different form; it's not enough to make declarations at conferences. It would be worth considering what other forms such solidarity could take.'

Doris Jäger

'Nearer to life'

'Each day thousands of women realise what they have to do: defend life in a society in which death gives the orders...'

'We all bear responsibility for what happens around us. We have to defend ourselves, to be constantly talking to others and warning them. Even if we aren't mayors or priests, we have a very special sort of power.'

The first quote comes from Dona Maria[1], aged 60, who lives in Mauá in São Paulo, and the second one from Sylvia, aged 35, a housewife and mother from Biblis, a small German town dominated by a nuclear power station. Although at first glance these women appear to come from entirely different worlds — one from Brazil, where the struggle for survival itself often dominates everyday life, and one from Germany, where economically at least everything seems to be under control — they have very much in common. Both are women who are putting up a fight in their own corners of the world. In Brazil, they fight against hunger, inadequate health care and a defective infrastructure; in Germany, among other things, against the menace unleashed by nuclear power. And neither is unique, a lone combatant, for they are both fighting in concert with others — and largely with other women.

When I lived in Brazil I often wondered why it is that the people who battle so resolutely for change and against the injustice which they see around them are generally women. On my return to Germany I lived for two years in Biblis and my experiences there were very similar. For once again it was first and foremost women who were not prepared to accept the nuclear power station in Biblis, with all its attendant ideology, without an argument. After I had lived there for a while and become a member of the group, I realised that their resistance took a very similar form to that of Brazilian women and was also justified in similar ways. I should like to put a few of these points up for discussion in the form of four theses. In order to illustrate these theses, I will use quotations taken from tape-recorded interviews conducted with a number of women. One is an interview which I conducted with the members of a Housewives' Union (ADC) in Maurá in 1986. The ADC is a group of women who for several years have been calling for improvements in the deplorable social conditions in their area while at the same time looking in particular at those problems which specifically affect women, discussing them among themselves and together taking steps towards emancipation. The other interview took place in 1988 with a few of the women involved in the Women's and Mothers' Solidarity Group in Biblis (Hessen). These women have set themselves the task of making the local population aware, through a steady supply of information and regular actions at the site of the nuclear power station, of the threat which it poses and thereby of 'softening up' its almost monolithic bloc of supporters and beneficiaries.

Thesis 1: Women put up resistance because they are deeply involved in what is going on around them. They do not yield automatically to circumstantial pressures, but critically analyse any ideology which claims to explain and justify something of which they are unsure. Or, as Maria once put it, quite simply, '... somehow we are nearer to life...'

'Even while we were still at school we were always being "educated" about how clean, safe and necessary the nuclear power station was... they thought they'd get in early with their brain-washing. But somehow there was always an uneasiness there. And after Chernobyl we were able to express this openly and admit to our fears. We spoke to other women, who we thought would feel similarly. Then we got hold of some information, discussed it together and took it to the public. Very gradually we began to defend ourselves against the concentrated power of the nuclear power station's supporters... It would all be much simpler if people would admit to their fears, because only then will they discover that things can be changed.'

'A couple of years ago a lot of children died of meningitis in our area. It wasn't fate, as they would have had us believe, but because we had no sewage system. The hygiene conditions under which we were forced to live were intolerable. Why, we asked ourselves, do we pay our taxes and never get anything in return? We've analysed our day-to-day problems and recognised that their causes often have something to do with political decisions. By doing that we've become politicised in our attitudes to our everyday lives.'

Thesis 2: For a woman, taking steps towards organising with others and participating in resistance with other women is often part of her personal emancipation from a situation in which she is under the control of a husband or father.

'As I stood in front of the supermarket collecting signatures my father turned up to go shopping. When he saw me he turned round and went away... but I'd decided.'

'When I wanted to go away with our group last year, my husband and I regularly came to blows. That's because he thinks that a married woman shouldn't stay away from home overnight. They were really tough, those few days, but I won — it was my first step towards emancipation, you know?'

Thesis 3: When women organise in order to fight social injustice and oppression, they often find the courage to overcome society's expectations of them.

'Before my first demo I thought to myself, you can't go. I've been in the gymnastics club for years, both of my children are at school here... I thought, they'll really tear us off a strip. But then when I drove the banners there, I stayed with the other women after all. Several people said to me, "What, you're one of them too?" I must have been quite white. I was trembling. But when you've done it once you can do anything!'

'It is said time and again of us women that our role is to keep quiet and do our household chores. And because of this constant pressure I'd already reached the stage where I could hardly open my mouth in front of others. Even at school, when the children were involved in something, I couldn't talk sensibly. But with the help of this group I've learned to do it again. No one here jumped down my throat. I got more confident and now I can hold my own in public. We've grown together.'

Thesis 4: Women have more staying power because they appreciate the real value of what they are doing. Again and again they stress the fact that the purpose of their involvement is not to achieve an objective, but that they also consider it a success when women are brave enough to stand up and defend themselves together against injustice and oppression. This does not mean that their objective is not pursued resolutely; success is not defined, as we are used to defining it in our society, in terms of a particular achievement which can be measured, but is perceived when women start to say, 'We've enjoyed the struggle...'

'Clearly, the nuclear power station isn't going to be shut down in the near future. But that doesn't mean our work is pointless. We're raising consciousness! You know, when suddenly you see two people standing next to you at a demonstration who come from very traditional Biblis families and have always been frightened of expressing themselves publicly, then I see that as a success. That thrills me beyond belief...'

'Yes, we've got a sewage system now, but that isn't the most important thing. What's important to us is that people become aware of their situation, that they learn to recognise injustice and to defend themselves. We have to demand a little at a time, because that's the only way we'll get what's due to us...'

Doubtless I could find many more points to illustrate how similarly women reason and act in relation to organising and resistance. But completeness is not important here. What was important for me was to discover that our involvement — as women — is not 'restricted', but that by making ourselves aware of our day-to-day oppression and the dangers which we face we can turn them around together and defend ourselves against them, that we have already taken the first step towards solidarity with our sisters in the so-called Third World.

Carolin Winter-Burzeya

Sketches of a journey

Friday afternoon. A statement is being taken in the building occupied by the *Polícia Federal* São Paulo. To be precise, the police are questioning someone. The woman solicitor tries, in vain, to discourage the policeman's coarse manner by being friendly and accommodating. The policeman — an irascible man from the lower ranks, who is all the more ambitious as a result — gets to work.

He wants the names of all the women. When and where did they enter the country? What is the purpose of their trip? Present address? In the pose of a hero from a detective story, with legs dangling casually and an air of triumph, he gets down to details. 'You needn't bother denying it, we know anyhow. On Wednesday morning you spoke from the loudspeaker van owned by the metalworkers' union at Mercedes, and on Thursday at Volkswagen. And at lunchtime today you took part in a meeting in front of the Daiwa works.' He names names, places and times. They have a good control system — the Brazilian security forces in league with the multinationals.

The evening has begun. The interrogation ends. An entry is made in my passport, rendering the tourist visa granted four days ago invalid in 72 hours time. An arbitrary act, as later court proceedings will demonstrate.

The men who hold power in Brazil are not spiteful and are happy to forego further persecution. Nevertheless, the women's trip which began so energetically has become rather complicated. And just when we were beginning to get to know our hosts and hostesses in São Bernardo do Campo (São Paulo), a city full of multinational car-manufacturing companies and the cradle of the new trade union movement.

We had set out to put our own stamp, as women, on the direct contact which has been developing gradually since 1984 between German and Brazilian trade unionists working for large transnational companies like Mercedes and Volkswagen: given male dominance in German as well as Brazilian trade unions, particularly in the car industry, previous meetings and exchanges had been marked by a more or less total absence of women. Reason enough then for a few women activists employed by Daimler Benz to organise a trip of their own — with other interested parties — as a women's group.

We had prepared our trip thoroughly, taking advantage of the contacts which had already been built up with trade unionists in the São Bernardo metalworkers' trade union and on the Mercedes works committee. Letters containing suggestions for possible programmes, dates, accommodation and so on went to and fro. We planned, of course, to get together with our colleagues on the Mercedes works committee and in the trade union. Above all, we wanted to establish contact with women, to learn about their lives and their work in the factories, in the trade union movement, in local initiatives, in mothers' clubs and in other projects organised by the 'popular movements'.

Our colleagues on the Mercedes works committee were looking forward to this latest visit by a German delegation and awaited our women's group with interest. More importantly, women from the groups and projects which we wanted to learn about were excited at the prospect of an exchange with us. The women in the São Bernardo metalworkers' trade union had only recently established a women's committee.

Our arrival in this world left us with lasting and intense impressions and memories. Our first meeting takes place in Dulce's flat. Dulce is one of three women who put us up. She, Maria and Rita are married to men active in the trade union movement and employed by *Mercedes Benz do Brasil*. The three women themselves aren't in paid employment; their job is to run their homes, look after their children, and replenish their husbands' labour and fighting power. The three women normally take a back seat and see to whatever has to be done.

The conversation starts rather shyly. Our three hostesses don't know each other. But they do know each other's husbands from accounts given by their own husbands, all of whom sit on the works committee together. They start to talk about themselves, something they're not used to doing. We talk about their everyday lives as women. How they manage on their low incomes with Brazil's high inflation rate, the prices of various things, how much their rent or the mortgage repayments on their flats cost. Three times the minimum wage, which is what 70 per cent of those employed by Mercedes earn, isn't enough to support a family of four or five. The women have, somehow, to earn something extra.

Maria sells homemade pastries locally, Rita sells sweets. They'd both prefer proper paid jobs, but there are various reasons why there aren't any. For one thing, where would they leave their children? There are no affordable children's day nurseries. For another, even in the industrial region in which they live they wouldn't find jobs. As a rule companies just don't take on married women of child-bearing age or with small children.

Dulce and Rita in particular would like jobs so as not to get bogged down in housework and childcare, which they see as somewhat restrictive. Dulce does a certain amount of work in the community. Rita also used to be active an that area, along with her husband. She hasn't kept it up, but it might be an idea. Slowly we find things which unite us: we agree that it's important for women to do something themselves and for themselves and not simply to support their husbands in their activities.

Germans Gabi and Angelika are married to 'Mercedes men' active in the union, and both know what it means for union activities to take priority over family life, in the evenings and at the weekend, when their husbands' interest and support are required. Angelika works part-time as a secretary, Gabi as a housewife, like the Brazilian women. Despite the similarity in their situations, there are many differences: the Brazilian women's lower incomes, the danger that their husbands might be dismissed because of their union activities, the limited ability to fall back on welfare services.

The morning ends cheerfully with a shared meal enhanced by a selection of European cheeses. Two days later our hostesses come with us to meet the São Bernardo women's committee, while their husbands look after the children.

The São Bernardo and Diadema women's committee is a federation of various women's groups from the region. Women from the urban mothers' clubs and women's societies are represented, as are woman trade unionists from the CUT and individual trade unions, woman metalworkers, women working in the chemical industry, women who have joined forces in the housewives' union, and the women who have recently opened the independent *Nora Astorga* women's centre — a place in which to hold feminist discussions, where they can provide alternative health care (with gynaecological advice, self-help groups etc.) and where they eventually hope to set up an arts and crafts co-operative. The women's committee provides mutual support and coordinates joint actions, for example on the 8th of March.

That evening we plan a joint public women's protest outside the Japanese metal company Daiwa Sangyo for the coming Friday. Women trade unionists have discovered in a roundabout way that the woman workers in this only recently-opened metal factory have been subjected to highly undignified treatment.

As a result of the factory's sanitary facilities having once been soiled with blood, the company called all its woman employees to a meeting at which the women were harshly rebuked for their lack of tidiness and cleanliness and were described as 'filthy pigs' and 'obscene'. In addition, all the company's woman workers were subjected to detailed questioning in an attempt to find out which of them was having a period. Finally, the company presented all the women in the factory with a questionnaire which it described as an opinion poll aimed at improving cleanliness and discipline in the washing and changing rooms and to which the women were told to put their names. It contained the following questions:

1. Do you have a bathroom of your own at home?
2. Do you have a toilet at home?
3. Should the company install different models of toilet?
4. When do you have your period: from... to...?
5. How long does it last, approximately ... days?
6. Do you use any protection, for example tampons or towels?
7. Do you normally shower more than once a day during your period?
8. Do you get cramps during your period?
9. Do you take any medication for them?
10. What?
11. Have you ever been to a gynaecologist?
12. Would a litre of ethanol by the toilet solve the hygiene problems?
13. Name someone to be responsible for the sanitary facilities.
14. Your suggestions for improving hygiene:

To punish the women for soiling the toilets, the company brought in rules whereby in future two woman workers would have to make sure the washrooms were tidy each day at the end of their shift and women wishing to use the toilets would have to fetch the key from the foreman. The women trade unionists told us that this regime — like examinations or questioning about periods — is one of the methods widely used by companies to keep their woman workers under better control.

Naturally we are keen to accompany the women from the São Bernardo women's committee and the CUT to their public protest outside the gates of the Japanese factory.

When 11am on Friday — the start of the factory lunch break — comes, there are not all that many people around. The Women's union from the Inamar area of the town has brought its banner, which reads *Estamos presentes*. The oldest of its activists, a

62-year-old woman, has proudly set it up next to her. 'Of course, I'm always here', she says, 'We have to make headway, don't we?'

The speakers have taken up their positions on the loud speaker van. The demonstration begins. The events which have taken place in the factory are publicly condemned. Marcia gives a fiery speech. She is heavily pregnant, which gives her words a certain persuasive power: 'Ladies, we cannot accept this. We have to defend ourselves against attacks, against being patronised and against discrimination! How disgraceful to insult women because of their menstrual blood. It is the most normal thing in the world, this blood. No man sees the light of day without having it on his body. So, please ladies, let's not allow ourselves to be browbeaten. We must organise and stand up for our rights. That is why we are in the union.'

The women workers leave the factory building for the lunch break timidly, without showing any sign that they are paying attention. Some of them hurry from the site to their nearby homes, others sit themselves down somewhere in the shadow of the factory.

The union's loud speaker system drenches the whole area in sound and proves exceedingly penetrating — certainly reaching every boss's office. We are asked, as we have been at union meetings at Volkswagen and Mercedes over the last few days, to say a few words. Hella, a works committee member practiced in public speaking, accepts. In a brief message of greeting to the factory's women workers she first calls on the bosses to come out and discuss these misogynistic events. 'But since they're not likely to do that', she continues, 'I should like to wish all the women here the very best of luck in their struggle.' Next Gabi says a few words of greeting: 'In Germany, too, women earn less than men and there's a shortage of nursery schools. I admire the courage and the strength of the women of Brazil.'

Would we still have made these speeches if we had foreseen that the company would call the São Paulo police? We have often asked ourselves the same question. The Brazilian trade unionists were, just as surprised as we were when in the afternoon the police showed up at the union's headquarters to question us... Until then foreign delegations had always been able to pass on greetings at union meetings unhindered. Was it something to do with the firm being new, with the Japanese method of dealing with the trade union movement in general, or with the fact that it was women who had so shamefully and publicly placed the company's treatment of menstrual blood on the agenda and in doing so reviled the company?

'Well, now you have discovered for yourselves the conditions under which we must struggle and how the tiniest little thing, like just speaking in public, is suppressed here', say the Brazilian women as we are forced to tussle with the Aliens' Registration Office, a section of the police force. Without choosing to, we have learned from all this what it means to be on their side, to take up a joint position. There or here. These shared experiences add to the intensity of our exchange.

During visits we get to know some of the women's organisations which make up the São Bernardo women's committee — like the Inamar Women's Union — better. Inamar is one of Brazil's countless *bairros populares* (working class areas). In the sweltering midday heat we arrive, after an arduous search, at the Union's headquarters, a relatively large building, formerly a garage, which the town of Diadema leases to the women members for a peppercorn rent. We are expected. The women have put out chairs in a circle in one corner of the room. Elsewhere in the room there is a sewing class underway, with 20 women taking part, and in every other available space there are children romping. The lorries thundering past in the street make a deafening roar which makes the shed's metal walls shake.

We all introduce ourselves: age, married or not, children or not, working or not. That is the basis for what comes later. Then we are told a little about the Union: the women of Inamar first came together as a local women's group in order to demand a health centre. And they got it too!

At first they met in individual members' houses, but that was always too cramped. Gradually they had the idea of finding a room of their own and founding a society, and managed to get the backing of the municipal authorities. Now the women have a regular venue for the courses they run sewing courses and others dealing with health issues — and for their meetings, at which they discuss how best to make progress in their campaign for the long-overdue establishment of a crèche in their area. It is one of many demands.

We ask a lot of questions about the courses. How their work is financed, their prospects of finding a better building, and finally whether their husbands support or just tolerate their work here. No one really wants to answer that one: 'Well, it's not too bad.'

The conversation seems to be petering out. Finally, the chairwoman takes a deep breath. 'Well, I'd like to say something. I'm a member of the Workers' Party and was recently elected to go to the delegates' congress, where everything is decided. Just before the congress I got a voting card. And when I went home with it my husband tore it up because he didn't want me to go to meetings like that, here or at any congress. I didn't know what to do. I didn't really want to go without the card, because I knew I wouldn't be able to vote, just listen. In the end I went anyway and told the girls who were organising it what had happened, and got a new card and was able to take part properly and vote.'

Now all the women start to talk about their relationships with their husbands, some of whom support their activities more or less while others just support their activities less.

We'd had experience of that too. 'My husband was very conservative', says Hella. 'Whenever I went to union meetings he used to say it was all a load of rubbish anyway. In the end I divorced him.' The practical aspects of this interest the Brazilian women greatly. 'How many children have you got? Yes, with one child it's just about possible, but with four, which is what I have, it's more difficult. And here that also wouldn't work because we don't have enough money. We just don't earn enough. So here it's more usual for couples to stay together. When the children are older, then perhaps. But I often say to him, Look, I've done the housework, seen to the children, now there's no reason why I shouldn't go to the women's meeting. Anyway, it's for our area.'

The women tell us that they are gradually gaining more freedom and describe the kinds of resistance they come up against. 'When we were collecting signatures locally for the health centre, one man told me he wouldn't sign because the action was being organised by the Women's Union. So I asked him whether he couldn't at least think of his children for once. There are men who don't feel any responsibility at all.'

We also get around to the subject of contraception. Whether in Germany men see to it, or whether it's the woman's responsibility there too, and whether in Germany the main form of contraception is sterilisation.

Time moves on — the meeting continues in one of the women's homes. First we see the collective food store, the women are involved in the Community Shopping Movement organised by the popular movement in São Paulo. All the women's unions in a particular area of the town get together to buy basic foodstuffs direct from the producers or from a wholesaler and organise its resale to signed-up members. It isn't only another way of reducing the cost of living, it also helps the women's unions to organise better — in all aspects of their work. And that's important, especially for women, who tend to spend most of their time in the neighbourhood. We talk for a long time — over cakes and drinks, and after Antónia has shown us her entire home.

During our conversations with Brazilian women we find we have a lot in common, although their living conditions are so different from our own. We feel a bond being created at our meetings and we can build bridges on the basis of our experiences, both those we share and those which are different. There is enrichment in this and a broadening and sharpening of our outlook and our involvement.

Although we have not yet managed to carry out our plan to invite the Brazilian women to visit us in Germany, we still maintain our contacts in Brazil in a variety of ways.

Cordula Stucke

Glossary

ADC

Associação de Donas de Casa
Housewives' Union

Associação de Mulheres de Inamar
Inamar Women's Union

bairro popular

see *favela*

bóia-fria

Day labourer. Literally, 'the worker's lunch-box'; a term used to describe day labourers, male and female, most of whom live on the outskirts of towns and are hired by labour contractors to work on the land on a daily basis.

carteira de trabalho

Employment papers. An employee's record book issued to every worker for employment purposes. It must be presented to each new employer, and records employment dates as well as wages and social welfare contributions paid. However, at least half the country's unskilled labourers do not have a *carteira* and are employed illegally, without employment rights.

CNQMT

Commissão da Questão da Mulher Trabalhadora
Commission for Women's Issues

comissão de fábrica

Works committee. Works committees are employees' representative bodies elected by the workforce at factory level. They are just one of the achievements of Brazil's new trade union movement, which used union 'committees' at factory level to organise the huge strikes which took place after 1978. Subsequently demand grew for official regulations governing works committees, the main purpose being to secure protection against unlawful dismissal for trade unionists active in representing the workers' interests. The unions succeeded in concluding agreements with a few companies (almost exclusively multinationals in the São Paulo area) on setting up works committees. Brazil's works committees are, in general, much worse off than their Western European counterparts in terms of the workers' rights to participate in decision-making, to be involved in the running of the company and to information, and in terms of the number of members permitted, members' rights to carry out duties in work time, resources etc.

companheira Female colleague or comrade. Not a martial or militant term, but an affectionate, familiar term for a female fellow-combatant, someone who is 'one of the crowd' and towards whom one feels a sisterly attachment.

consciência Consciousness. *conscientização* (consciousness-raising) *Tomar consciência* (to become conscious) is a common expression in Brazilian Portuguese. It does not suggest the slightly resonant idealistic excess implied in some languages, but means 'to become aware', of something, of the way people live, of oneself. *Conscientização* is a related, equally routine term. It is an important part of Paulo Freire's theory of education and therefore also of *educação popular* (popular education) as a whole. The word contains the elements 'consciousness' and 'action', and accordingly 'raising someone's consciousness' is regarded as a process which takes place in conjunction with some kind of practical action *Conscientizaçao* as it relates to 'becoming conscious' is often defined in terms of 'growing'.

CONTAG *Confederação Nacional de Trabalhadores na Agricultura* National Confederation of Farmworkers

CUT *Central Única dos Trabalhadores* Central Workers' Organisation. The CUT was founded in 1983 and is Brazil's independent trade union umbrella organisation. In founding this unified umbrella organisation the trade unions gained a certain measure of trade union freedom and independence from the state. The unions had been under state control since the 1930s and meetings at anything higher than branch level were prohibited.

favela Urban slum settlement. *Bairro popular* (working-class quarter) *Favela* is the Brazilian term for the urban slum settlements in which the majority of the poor, in particular the black population, lives. The first Brazilian *favelas* were started in the last century in Rio de Janeiro by the survivors of the war against Paraguay. More were begun by former slaves following the abolition of slavery. Since then these areas have been growing steadily as the population has become increasing impoverished. *Favelas* are generally created through the occupation (*invasões*) of unused land, and some gradually develop, after years or even decades of attempted urbanisation and of trying to become part of the urban infrastructure, into *bairros populares* (working-class quarters).

IBGE

Instituto Brasileiro de Geografia e Estatística
Brazilian Institute of Geography and Statistics

jeito

Luck, skill, solutions, favours. In fact, there is no direct translation for the term *jeito*. It is a metaphor for the Brazilian way of life, the ability to find an unconventional solution, even in seemingly hopeless situations, straightforwardly, with a little help from chance, but in particular as a result of resolute attempts at enlisting the support of others and of exploiting contacts. To do someone a favour is accordingly also described as *jeito*. You do not get far in Brazil without it. Its negative side is the reduction of rights to favours.

machismo

A phenomenon known the world over whereby the male of the species seeks to reinforce his dominance.

Macumba

An Afro-Brazilian religion.

Movimento Custo da Vida
Cost of Living Movement

Movimento Feminino Pela Anistia
Women's Amnesty Movement

Movimento de Luta por Creches
Fight for Creches Movement

MMT

Movimento das Mulheres Trabalhadores Rurais
Women Farmworkers' Movement

MNU

Movimento Negro Unificado
United Black Movement

MST

Movimento dos Sem-Terra
Movement for Landless Families

município

District. An administrative area: a rural district.

OAB	*Ordem de Advogados Brasileiros* Brazilian Bar Association
PAISM	*Programa de Assistência Integral a Saúde da Mulher* Integrated Women's Health Programme
PDT	*Partido Democrático Trabalhista* Democratic Workers' Party, a social-democrat party and member of the Socialist International, strongest Janeiro.
PMDB	*Partido Movimento Democrático Brasileiro* Party of the Brazilian Democratic Movement, the former opposition alliance from the time of the military dictatorship which consisted of various left-wing to liberal parties.
PT	*Partido dos Trabalhadores* Workers' Party, the grassroots party of the new socialist movement.
pastoral	Pastoral commission. The Catholic Church has various 'pastoral commissions' or 'church working groups', each concerned with a different occupation. They are organised regionally, nationally and at federal state level and tackle the specific problems encountered by different sections of the population. The groups' organisation by occupation is of great importance when it comes to coordinating local activities which are 'occupation or target group specific'. There is, for example, a *pastoral da terra* (a support group for landless peasants), a *pastoral operária* (a support group for workers), a fishermen's support group and an Indians' support group.
povo	The people. The term *povo* does not suggest any ethnic or racist racial definition of society, as is the case, for example, with the German word *Volk*, nor any definition of society based on territorial or national considerations. Instead, the *povo* is a social group, and the term denotes the equality in class terms of broad sections of the population. *Povo* means 'the peoples' classes' as opposed to 'the ruling classes', 'the common people' as opposed to 'the rich', 'the plebeians' as opposed to 'the oligarchy'.

salário mínimo

Minimum wage. The minimum wage system was introduced with Brazil's labour legislation in the 1930s. The minimum wage is set by the government on the basis of a shopping basket of commodities and is supposed to cover the minimum requirements of a family of four. In fact, the basis on which it is calculated, which changes constantly, does not even vaguely reflect those minimum requirements. In theory all employees covered by labour law have to be paid at least the minimum wage, and wages must not fall below this level. The minimum wage for a 44-hour week varies between US$50-100 a month, depending on inflation. In wage negotiations the minimum wage level is used as a fixed standard for comparison: employers pay half minimum wages, two times the minimum wage, ten times the minimum wage and so on.

The writers

Maria Cecília Camargo, born in 1958 in Brazil, studied economics, working in Heidelberg since 1988 on the 'Frontier Internships in Mission' programme, worked on a project entitled 'Brazilian women working for German companies in Brazil'.

Christiane Fröhlich, born in 1962, theologian in Berlin, grew in a commune; showed particular interest in women's issues during a 14-month stay in Brazil.

Erika Füchtbauer, born in 1964, feminist, lived for a year and a half in Brazil with day-labourers, now living in Berlin.

Loreley Garcia, born in 1956, sociologist, has a masters in political science, doctoral candidate in philosophy, PT activist, single mother of two: lives in São Paulo.

Dorothea Hillingshäuser, born in 1962, theologian in Hamburg, spent three months in Brazil, mainly in the Northeast, where she was in contact with women farmworkers and other women.

Doris Jäger, born in 1958, bookseller and theologian, has spent two long periods in Brazil, lecturer at the UNI-POP (Universidade Popular) in Belém, Pará, since August 1990.

Gerborg Meister, born in 1948, studied economic and social sciences, now a lecturer at the Comenius-Theological College in Mettinyen, co-editor of the *Brasilien-Nachrichten*, Osnabrück, has visited Brazil on several occasions.

Gerdi Nützel, born in 1961, theologian in Berlin, has taken part in several study-tours, spent 15 months in Brazil in 1988/89; specialisms: women and the world economy and woman theologians of the Federal Republic of Germany, the German Democratic Republic and Brazil.

Helga Oberländer, born in 1947, social worker, lives with her husband and child in Hamburg, worked for three years in the Northeast of Brazil, mainly with women; experience in street theatre.

Anna Lúcia Florisbela dos Santos, born in 1951 in Niteroi/Rio de Janeiro, studied economics in Brazil; a member of Brazil's Black Movement since 1972, has worked in Guinea-Bissau, in the Cape

Verde Islands and in the Dominican Republic; in Darmstadt since 1985.

Susanne Schultz, born in 1964, has twice visited Brazil, went on a three-month visit to the women's health centre SOS Corpo in Recife in 1989, studied political science in Berlin.

Petra Sorge, born in 1957, has visited Brazil many times, *capoeirista*, lambada dancer, works on education for the unemployed in Germany and is involved in projects which unite women, previously in Hamburg, nowadays world-wide, present specialism: racism/sexism.

Cordula Stucke, born in 1954, studied psychology, education and political science, works at the head office of 'Equality for Women' in Hamburg; has visited Brazil many times, is involved in developing German/Brazilian trade union contacts at grassroots level.

Carolin Winter-Burzeya, born in 1961, student of evangelical theology, mother of two, spent 1985/86 in São Paulo where she worked with 'action groups', specialisms: women and trade unions. After returning to Germany, used her experience as the basis of seminars and work with project groups.

Resources and Action

UK and Ireland

AMNESTY INTERNATIONAL is a worldwide organisation working for human rights. In Brazil it has taken up cases like that of Edmeia Da Silva Eugenio, killed in Rio de Janeiro in January 1993 while campaigning with a group of mothers for an investigation into the disappearance of their sons, allegedly kidnapped by the police.
British Section, 99-119 Rosebery Avenue, London EC1R 4RE
International Secretariat, 1 Easton Street, London WC1X 8DJ

BRAZIL NETWORK links individuals and organisations in the UK working on Brazil and interested in keeping informed about events there. It publishes a quarterly newsletter.
PO Box 1325, London SW9 0RA

BRAZIL SOLIDARITY GROUP in Ireland aims to generate interest in and awareness of Brazil; to learn from Brazilian experiences of development and to campaign on specific issues affecting Brazil.
c/o Stephen McCarthy, 1 Ashfield Park, Ballymount Lane, Tallaght, Dublin 24, Ireland

CAFOD (the Catholic Fund for Overseas Development) supports mobilisation, networking and training of grassroots rural and urban women's organisations in all regions of Brazil. This programme includes trade unions of domestic workers, the Rural Women Workers' Movement, women's popular housing associations, the church's Pastoral Programme for Marginalised Women, women's shelters, women working with street children and AIDS projects.
2 Romero Close, Stockwell Road, London SW9 9TY

CHRISTIAN AID has given priority to independent women's organisations in rural areas and in poor districts of cities. In rural areas in Brazil it supports women among the landless and peasant farming communities; in the cities washer-women, women factory workers, women in the *favelas*, prostitutes and girls living on the streets.
Apart from supporting women's organisations, it supports more general activities on gender relations, especially in the area of advice and training.
PO Box 100, London SE1 7RT

OXFAM has two main objectives in its work in Brazil — to strengthen women's organisations at a grassroots and national level, and to encourage other project partners working in different spheres to include gender issues in planning their work.
274 Banbury Road, Oxford OX2 7DZ

SAVE THE CHILDREN has had a Brazil programme since 1990, concentrating in the major urban centres. Key priorities are support for organisations working on children's rights, including support for the street children's movement, community schools and educational work on HIV/AIDS.

17 Grove Lane, London SE5 8RD

SCIAF (Scottish Catholic International Aid Fund) supports women's initiatives worldwide. In Brazil it provides financial support for specific women's programmes, as well as engaging in constant dialogue with all its partners there to further the common understanding of gender issues and the development process. Examples of SCIAF-supported programmes include the breastfeeding promotion group ORIGEM in Recife/Olinda and the Network of Rural Working Women (AMMTR) of five southern states.

5 Oswald Street, Glasgow G1 4QR

TROCAIRE has partnerships with women's groups in Brazil in both the project funding and development education areas. The Irish Trade Unions/Trocaire partnership has links in particular with the Domestic Workers' Union.

169 Booterstown Avenue, Co Dublin, Ireland

WOMANKIND WORLDWIDE supports women's groups in developing countries both through direct funding and by raising awareness in the UK of their needs and concerns. Recent grants in Brazil have been for campaigning and training in relation to violence, and the continued support of Passage House, a refuge for street girls in Recife.

122 Whitechapel High Street, London E1 7PT

USA

AMERICAN FRIENDS SERVICE COMMITTEE runs a small women's health programme in *favelas* on the periphery of São Paulo.

1414 Cherry Street, Philadelphia, PA 19102

AMERICAS WATCH has published reports on violence against Brazilian women.

1522 K Street NW, Washington, DC 20005

AMNESTY INTERNATIONAL USA published a report *Women in the Front Line: Human Rights Violations Against Women* in 1991 on human rights violations against women in Brazil and many other countries.

322 Eighth Avenue, New York, NY 10001

BRAZIL NETWORK (USA) publishes a newsletter, *Contato*, with articles on Brazilian women and many other issues. The Network also sponsors tours and visits by Brazilian activists and publishes occasional reports on social questions.

815 15th Street NW, Suite 426, Washington, DC 20009

Several private consulting firms administer health and family-planning projects funded by the US Agency for International Development (USAID). The Futures Group administers GENESYS, a USAID project that assists local non-governmental organisations working with women's groups in the Brazilian Amazon.

GENESYS Project, 1050 17th Street NW, Suite 1000, Washington, DC 20036

Further Reading

Out of the Shadows: Women, Resistance and Politics in South America

Jo Fisher

Interviews with women activists in Argentina, Chile, Paraguay and Uruguay provide a unique insight into the rise of the women's movement under military dictatorship, and the challenges posed by the return to civilian government.

'Her faithful recording of women's voices will bring a new science of society and history into being.' June Nash, City College, New York, editor of *Sex and Class in Latin America*

1993   £9.00/US$17.00   228 pages   ISBN 0 906156 77 7

Brazil: War on Children

Gilberto Dimenstein

Interweaves first hand reportage, interviews and statistics to paint a picture of life for Brazil's street children. The author describes a world of pimps, muggers, prostitutes and petty criminals; homeless children who live in fear of sudden death at the hands of the off-duty police and other vigilantes who make up Brazil's death squads.

1991   £5.75/US$12.00   88 pages   ISBN 0 906156 62 9

Fight for the Forest: Chico Mendes in his own words

Chico Mendes and Tony Gross

Chico Mendes, charismatic founder of the Brazilian rubber tappers' union talks of his life's work in what was to be the last major interview before his assassination. He recalls the rubber tappers' campaign against forest clearances and their alliances with local Indians and the international environmental lobby. Together they developed sustainable alternatives for the Amazon which would guarantee both their livelihoods and the forest's future.

1989   £5.75/US$12.00   128 pages   ISBN 0 906156 68 8

The above prices are for paperback editions and include post and packing. Write for a free LAB books catalogue to Latin America Bureau, 1 Amwell Street, London EC1R 1UL

LAB books are distrbuted in North America by Monthly Review Press, 121 West 27 Street, New York, NY 10001

The Latin America Bureau is an independent research and publishing organisation. It works to broaden public understanding of issues of human rights and social and economic justice in Latin America and the Caribbean.